THE NEW BIG BOOK OF HOCKEY FUN!

Project Editor: Ronnie Shuker
Art Direction: Leanne Gilbert
Cover Design: Leanne Gilbert
Graphic Design: Colin Elliott
Photo Research: Shea Berencsi
Photo Retouching: Éric Lépine
Puzzlemaker: Larry Humber

EXCLUSIVE DISTRIBUTOR:

For Canada and the United States:
Simon & Schuster Canada
166 King Street East, Suite 300
Toronto, ON M5A 1J3
Phone: (647) 427-8882
        1-800-387-0446
Fax: (647) 430-9446
simonandschuster.ca

Cover Information:
Matthews: Mark Blinch/NHLI via Getty Images
McDavid: Andy Devlin/NHLI via Getty Images
Subban: John Russell/NHLI via Getty Images
Laine (Back Cover): Jamie Sabau/NHLI via Getty Images

Catalogue data available from Bibliothèque
et Archives nationales du Québec

11-17

Printed in Canada

© 2017, Juniper Publishing,
division of the Sogides Group Inc.,
a subsidiary of Québecor Média Inc.
(Montreal, Quebec)

Legal deposit: 2017
National Library of Quebec
National Library of Canada

ISBN 978-1-988002-69-9

 Conseil des Arts   Canada Council
du Canada   for the Arts

We gratefully acknowledge the support of the Canada
Council for the Arts for its publishing program.

We acknowledge the financial support of the Government of
Canada through the Book Publishing Industry Development
Program (BPIDP) for our publishing activities.

THE NEW Hockey News BIG BOOK OF HOCKEY FUN!

The Hockey News

EDITED BY RONNIE SHUKER

JUNIPER
PUBLISHING
A Quebecor Media Corporation

INTRODUCTION

After the 2004-05 lockout, the hockey gods blessed fans with two new superstars, as Alex Ovechkin and Sidney Crosby arrived in the NHL at the same time. They were drafted first overall in 2004 and 2005, respectively, and neither disappointed in 2005-06. Both had more than 100 points as rookies and were neck-and-neck for the Calder Trophy all season long.

The 2016-17 season featured the best rookie crop since 'Sid' and 'Ovie' more than a decade ago. This time, it was Auston Matthews and Patrik Laine making all the headlines and highlights as the two went goal-for-goal throughout the season. Matthews (40) ended up edging Laine (36) in goals to win the Calder, the first in the history of the Toronto Maple Leafs.

But Matthews and Laine weren't the only rookies who took the league by storm in 2016-17. Toronto's other young guns William Nylander and Mitch Marner finished tied for third in rookie scoring with 61 points each, while Sebastian Aho, who grew up a rink rat in Finland watching his dad play in the SM-liiga, surprised everyone with 49 points on the Carolina Hurricanes. Matthew Tkachuk, son of former NHLer and 500-goal scorer Keith Tkachuk, finished with 48 points for the Calgary Flames and took a page out of his father's playbook by making enemies around the league. Zach Werenski of the Columbus Blue Jackets had the sixth-most points (47) ever by a rookie teenage defenseman in NHL history. Anthony Mantha, grandson of Montreal Canadiens legend Andre Pronovost, who won four straight Stanley Cups with the Habs from 1957 to 1960, scored 17 goals in just 60 games for the Detroit Red Wings. Jakob Chychrun, son of former NHL defenseman Jeff Chychrun, established himself as a regular on the Arizona Coyotes blueline as an 18-year-old. And then there was Ivan Provorov, who had the most ice time on the Philadelphia Flyers, something none of his fellow freshman accomplished on their teams.

The New Big Book of Hockey Fun, the follow-up to the first edition in 2014, pays tribute to 10 of the NHL's newest stars with profiles on their rise to fame and (soon) fortune. Yet these rookies weren't the league's only new recruits in 2016-17. Before the season began, the NHL announced that Las Vegas would be home to its next freshman franchise. The Vegas Golden Knights were thus born, and they quickly became the talk of the town all season long.

With that in mind, we inserted Vegas into our NHL teams section of the book, where we showcase the NHL's 31 clubs in 2016-17. Every one of them has an intro, a stats pack and a parade of puzzles, quizzes and activities for young fans of any team.

But that's not all. Behind the poetry on the ice is the science of the sport. Any fan who has ever wondered how sticks and pucks are made, how goalie masks are created and designed or how the heck a Zamboni actually works will find those answers here…and more. For all you plucky pucksters out there, hoping to become the next Matthews or Laine, we've included a collection of training articles on how to train like a pro, including tips and techniques from the game's best strength and conditioning coaches.

We start with Auston Matthews, who was even better with a bat than he is with a stick.

CONTENTS

4   INTRODUCTION

SUPERSTARS
8   AUSTON MATTHEWS
12   PATRIK LAINE
16   WILLIAM NYLANDER
20   ZACH WERENSKI
24   MITCH MARNER
28   IVAN PROVOROV
32   SEBASTIAN AHO
36   ANTHONY MANTHA
40   MATTHEW TKACHUK
44   JAKOB CHYCHRUN
48   FABULOUS FRESHMEN

TEAMS
52   ANAHEIM DUCKS
56   ARIZONA COYOTES
60   BOSTON BRUINS
64   BUFFALO SABRES
68   CALGARY FLAMES
72   CAROLINA HURRICANES
76   CHICAGO BLACKHAWKS
80   COLORADO AVALANCHE
84   COLUMBUS BLUE JACKETS
88   DALLAS STARS
92   DETROIT RED WINGS
96   EDMONTON OILERS
100   FLORIDA PANTHERS
104   LOS ANGELES KINGS

108   MINNESOTA WILD
112   MONTREAL CANADIENS
116   NASHVILLE PREDATORS
120   NEW JERSEY DEVILS
124   NEW YORK ISLANDERS
128   NEW YORK RANGERS
132   OTTAWA SENATORS
136   PHILADELPHIA FLYERS
140   PITTSBURGH PENGUINS
144   SAN JOSE SHARKS
148   ST. LOUIS BLUES
152   TAMPA BAY LIGHTNING
156   TORONTO MAPLE LEAFS
160   VANCOUVER CANUCKS
164   VEGAS GOLDEN KNIGHTS
168   WASHINGTON CAPITALS
172   WINNIPEG JETS

THE SCIENCE OF HOCKEY
178   HOW DOES A ZAMBONI WORK?
180   HOW ARE PUCKS MADE?
182   HOW ARE STICKS MADE?
184   HOW ARE GOALIE MASKS MADE?
186   HOW ARE GOALIE MASKS DESIGNED?
188   HOW SHOULD KIDS PRACTISE ON THE ICE?
190   HOW SHOULD KIDS TRAIN OFF THE ICE?
192   HOW MUCH HOCKEY SHOULD KIDS PLAY?

194   SOLUTIONS

SUPER

STARS
IN THE MAKING

TEN OF THE NHL'S TOP YOUNG GUNS TOOK THE NHL BY STORM IN 2016-17. EVERY ONE OF THEM HAD THE SAME DREAM: TO MAKE THE NHL. BUT THEY ALL TOOK DIFFERENT PATHS TO GET THERE

AUSTON #34 MATTHEWS

TORONTO MAPLE LEAFS

20, C, DRAFTED 1ST ROUND, 1ST OVERALL, IN 2016

BY KEN CAMPBELL & RYAN KENNEDY

The first time Morgan Rielly dropped in on Auston Matthews' condo in Toronto, he found plastic forks and paper plates, with the owner sitting on the couch playing video games. The funny thing is, though, for as much as Auston plays video games, Rielly claims Auston is by far the worst Call of Duty player on the team. "He's terrible," Rielly said. "It's his focus. He tends to wander a little bit, so you tend to lose him halfway through a game, then he comes back and then you lose him again. It's crazy how he can just be this laidback guy, but then he gets to the rink and he's one of the best players in the world."

This assessment doesn't surprise Brian Matthews one bit. In fact, he claims that his son was even better at baseball than hockey growing up, which makes perfect sense since he grew up in Arizona. Auston played first and third base, but the pace of the game just wasn't for him. His father urged his children to play two sports. Baseball was a natural. After all, Brian was a pitcher, a pretty good one at Arizona, until he hurt his shoulder in the days before pitch counts. Auston's grandfather played college basketball at Pepperdine, and his uncle Wes played for the Miami Dolphins. Four games, one catch for 20 yards.

A college pitcher who went on to play semipro, Brian loved to challenge his son in the batter's box, and the right-handed Brian had more than just fastballs in his arsenal against the left-batting Auston. Brian threw sinkers and filthy stuff fathers don't typically give sons. "I was throwing everything at

> ### "HE WAS A PHENOMENAL BASEBALL PLAYER. THE HAND-EYE COORDINATION WAS UNREAL. BUT IT WAS TOO SLOW FOR HIM."
>
> #### BRIAN MATTHEWS, AUSTON'S FATHER

him, mixing it up," Brian said. "He never knew what was coming, but his hand-eye co-ordination was uncanny."

Auston could hit the ball a ton, yet he chose hockey, a game that was completely foreign to his father but the one that held more appeal. Coaches told him there was

more money to be made on the diamond than the ice rink, but Auston wasn't having it. When time constraints forced him to choose between sports at 13, baseball lost out handily. "He was a phenomenal baseball player," Brian said. "The hand-eye coordination was unreal. But it was too slow for him. If he could have batted every 30 seconds, it might have been a different story. But that's not how the game is played."

Playing hockey in Arizona meant a lot of travel for Auston – first to Las Vegas and Los Angeles, then to destinations across the continent. But he didn't really know how good he was until he tried out for the Michigan-based U.S. National Team Development Program. A leg injury during his under-17 season kept him off the radar of mass audiences, though scouts who'd seen him raved about the kid. As an under-18 star, he broke the NTDP record books, putting up more points in one season than any player in program history. Auston ended up with 117 points in 60 games, surpassing Patrick Kane's record of 102 in 58 games.

Auston could have gone on to play major junior or college hockey, but he decided to turn pro at just 17 years old and test his skills against men in Switzerland's top league. There, he worked on rounding out

2016–17 STATS   GP 82 | G 40 | A 29 | PTS 69 | PIM 14

"HE'S A HUMBLE YOUNG MAN AND HE'S REALLY GROUNDED, BUT HE KNOWS HOW GOOD HE IS AND HOW GOOD HE CAN BE."

MORGAN RIELLY

his game, particularly the defensive side. Racking up points has never been difficult for Auston, though, and it wasn't a problem in Zurich, where he had 24 goals and 22 assists for 46 points in just 36 games. "When it came to the D-zone, there's positioning," Auston said. "But in the offensive zone they gave me a lot of freedom for creativity."

Next up for Auston was the NHL. After the Maple Leafs took him first overall in the 2016 draft, Auston immediately became Toronto's top center at just 19 years old. And he didn't disappoint, winning the Calder Trophy as the league's rookie of the year.

With the exception of winning faceoffs, there is nothing Auston wasn't able to do very well in 2016-17. Even when he went through a 13-game scoring drought, he was doing almost everything right. And in an era when puck possession is so important, Auston is one of the most valuable players in the league to his team. Right now. "You don't need to convince me, I've been saying that since the World Cup," Rielly said. "He's a humble young man and he's really grounded, but he knows how good he is and how good he can be."

The Leafs haven't had a rookie that has given its fan base so much promise since the last time they had a No. 1 overall pick in Wendel Clark in 1985. Auston finished with 40 goals and 69 points, breaking Clark's rookie record of 34 goals and Peter Ihnacak's rookie points record of 66. From the time he scored four goals in his first NHL game, he has made a seamless transition, proving he belongs not only in the best league in the world, but among the best players in the best league in the world. "I'm not surprised," Brian said. "I know the work he put in. I know the work he put in this summer and I know the work he's going to put in next summer. We've tried to raise all our kids that you either do something 100 percent or you're doing it half-assed. So do it 100 percent and when it's time to relax and goof off, then go goof off at 100 percent."

Auston's success hasn't surprised his old man. How about to No. 34 himself? "Honestly, not really," he said. "I know what I'm capable of."

PATRIK #29

19, RW, DRAFTED 1ST ROUND, 2ND OVERALL, IN 2016

BY JARED CLINTON

It takes somewhere around five centuries for aluminum to decompose. That means there are 490-odd years left for some dedicated Finnish hockey fans to get their hands on some precious pieces of memorabilia. The dig site is the backyard of the Laine household in Tampere, Finland, and soda can shrapnel is the treasure. Those fragments of old aluminum cans, bashed, battered and burst to bits by six ounces of rubber, are a reminder of where Patrik Laine began his path to becoming one of the best rookie scorers in recent memory.

Laine's shot, used to blast soda cans apart years ago, was the talk of the NHL in 2016-17. It's lethal, both in strength and accuracy, and it didn't get that way overnight, which is to say it's not Laine's gift so much as his passion project. In his backyard, on the ice and in every moment he could spare, Laine would shoot. And when he was tired, he would shoot again. He'd shoot until his hands bled, as they did while training this past summer, and then he'd shoot some more. "I had a net in our backyard and I spent many hours there every day, just shooting," Laine said. "When the coaches would blow the whistle and everyone would get water, I stayed and took shots to improve it."

Laine has long since graduated from smashing soda cans in his backyard, moving on to dominating the SM-liiga in Finland and now to destroying the already high expectations put upon him as an 18-year-old rookie in the NHL. On his first night in the league, Laine showed off the skills built

> ## "I WAS A BETTER GOALIE THAN A FORWARD, BUT I THINK I'M GOOD WITH MY FATHER'S DECISION."
> ### PATRIK LAINE

in his parents' backyard with a laser wrist shot from the left point that started a Jets comeback victory. He called his first NHL goal "the best moment in the world," made more special with his family there to see it. Days later, he had a hat trick in a showdown against Toronto Maple Leafs rookie Auston Matthews – the only player taken ahead of Laine in the 2016 draft – finished off by an overtime snipe that sent the MTS Centre into cheers. By the time 2016-17 ended,

Laine had scored 36 goals, seventh-most in the league.

The amazing thing in all of this, of course, is that Laine came close to spending his entire career trying to stop pucks. If Jets GM Kevin Cheveldayoff hasn't sent Laine's father, Harri, a thank you card yet, he may want to get out his finest stationary and draft up something special, because if it weren't for him, Laine might still be a goaltender somewhere in Finland. He didn't give up the position until he was 12. "I would have kept going but then my dad decided for me, and I went being a forward all the time," Laine said. "I was a better goalie than a forward, but I think I'm good with his decision."

That position change came only six years ago. Imagine what Laine could be capable of had he focused all his energy on scoring goals instead of stopping them. But there may be something to the connection between Laine's goaltending days and his current goal scoring ways. Facing Laine's shot hundreds of times already in practice, Jets goaltender Michael Hutchinson made note of a trait Laine has that few players, be it rookies or veterans, possess – the ability to use a goaltender's understanding of a shooter's tendencies against them. "He doesn't just

2016-17 STATS GP 73 | G 36 | A 28 | PTS 64 | PIM 26

"HE HAS NO PROBLEM SHOOTING FOR A REBOUND TO GET HIS TEAMMATES A GOAL, SHOOTING FIVE-HOLE OR PICKING A LOW CORNER OVER THE PAD. THAT'S MATURITY BEYOND HIS YEARS."

MICHAEL HUTCHINSON

pick the top corner every time," Hutchinson said. "A lot of kids, especially at 17 and 18 with a shot like that, want to come in and just shoot the puck as hard as they can and try to go bar down and blow one by the goalie every single time. He's not like that. He has no problem shooting for a rebound to get his teammates a goal, shooting five-hole or picking a low corner over the pad. That's maturity beyond his years."

It is impressive maturity given how swift his progression has been from goaltender to goal scorer. Laine is used to progressing quickly, though, because his six-year rise to becoming one of the world's best teenage players was preceded by a yearlong skyrocket up the draft rankings.

Laine had seven goals and 13 points in seven games at the 2016 world juniors en route to winning gold with Finland. He then returned to the Finnish League and dominated the post-season with 10 goals and 15 points as Tappara, his hometown team, captured the league title with Laine taking playoff MVP honors. His rapid rise continued at the World Championship in May, where he scored seven goals and 12 points on his way to a silver medal and yet another MVP honor. One month later, he was drafted second overall by the Jets.

It's sometimes forgotten that Laine is still a kid, and it's easy to see why. At 6-foot-5, 206 pounds, he's a teenager in a grown man's body. And if it's not Laine's size that makes us forget how young he is, it's his outspoken confidence that does. Laine has never shied away from being upfront about the fact he's a talented player. He openly stated he believed he had what it took to be the first-overall pick ahead of Matthews, he turned heads with his stick-twirling celebration and he has outright said he knows how good he is and he's not afraid to say it. That's a rare quality found in few players, and it has only increased his appeal. "I don't have to compare myself to anybody," Laine said. "Everybody is different, and I want to be me. I don't have to think about what everybody else has done. People can say what they want, but I just want to be me and create my own path."

WILLIAM #29 NYLANDER

TORONTO MAPLE LEAFS

20, RW, DRAFTED 1ST ROUND, 8TH OVERALL, IN 2014

BY KEN CAMPBELL

The day before the Maple Leafs hosted the Centennial Classic, they practiced ahead of the alumni game. With the large Toronto Argos dressing room to get dressed in, they arranged it so that every current Leaf had an alumni player on either side of him. It was no accident that Auston Matthews was beside Wendel Clark, and Mitch Marner was seated next to Doug Gilmour. Nikita Zaitsev sat between Bryan McCabe and his mentor, Dmitri Yushkevich. Zach Hyman between Darcy Tucker and Tie Domi? That works.

After practice, William Nylander, who was between Gary Roberts and Rick Vaive, spent much of the time getting signatures on a stick from the former Leafs. As a child of an NHL player, he'd grown up in NHL dressing rooms, yet here he was, indulging in a little hero worship. To be fair, though, his dad, Michael, played his last NHL game before William had reached his 12th birthday, so it's been a while. "Yeah, it was as a souvenir, but for sure, I want to know who those players are," Nylander said. "It's important to get to know the players who came before you. You want to learn about what they've been through…and you ask them what it was like when they were carrying the city. I tried to talk to them

about that and see what it was like when they were playing."

By the time William came into the world in 1996, Michael was an established NHLer. He had already been part of a blockbuster trade that had sent him from Hartford to

> ## "IT'S IMPORTANT TO GET TO KNOW THE PLAYERS WHO CAME BEFORE YOU. YOU WANT TO LEARN ABOUT WHAT THEY'VE BEEN THROUGH."
> ### WILLIAM NYLANDER

Calgary, where William was born, and had endured the first of three lockouts during career. And he wasn't even yet 24.

There are a lot of advantages to being a young father. For Michael, one of them came 16 years later when, like Gordie Howe, he had the chance to play professional hock-

ey with his son. It wasn't the NHL – actually it was the Allsvenskan, a division below the Swedish League – but it was a pro league, and Michael was proud of himself and his son. He played with William in Sodertalje in 2012-13 and the next season in Rogle. Most of the road trips were out and back the same day, but on the rare overnights, the father and son would room together. "Instead of dropping him off at the game, we all went together," Michael said. "When we played on the same line, it was just like another teammate…He was good enough as a young guy to play, and I was good enough as an old guy to play."

Michael played until they had to take the skates off him at 42, and that same passion was apparent early in his son's life. The father never had to instill a love for the game in William because it was always there. "I've always been pretty critical on both my boys…in a good way," Michael said. "Wherever William played, he was always up at the top with the other guys. You don't know how it's going to go when they get older, but he always kept that separation with the kids in his age group. He was playing with older guys, mostly."

In many ways, William is a hybrid of the North American and European systems. He

2016-17 STATS | **GP 81** | **G 22** | **A 39** | **PTS 61** | **PIM 32**

"WHEREVER WILLIAM PLAYED, HE WAS ALWAYS UP AT THE TOP WITH THE OTHER GUYS."

MICHAEL NYLANDER,
WILLIAM'S FATHER

played in Sweden, but his formative years of minor hockey were spent in the United States. He was a standout for the Chicago Mission bantam team in 2010-11, helping his team win a Silver Stick title (en route to MVP honors) and reach the national championship game. Michael recalled his son having to try out and compete against other kids from the age of seven to make teams, something that is foreign to Swedish players, who don't get really competitive about the game until they're 12 years old. "Here, you get used to competing in a different way and you never know if you're going to make the team," Michael said. "There is more competition for ice time."

William has taken the best of both worlds with him to the NHL. There are few players in the league who have better edges. He has abundant skills and is deadly on the power play. He had been playing with fellow rookies Matthews and Connor Brown but later in the season found a home on a line with Nazem Kadri and Leo Komarov. He has drawn the anger of his coach and even found himself in trade rumors. If the Leafs ever were in a position to better themselves on defense, it wouldn't be a stretch to suggest that any trading partner would want a young player such as William in return. He's an incomplete if promising project. "He's like everyone else. He's figuring out how to be a player in the NHL," said coach Mike Babcock. "He's obviously got good skills, good skill on the power play and 5-on-5, but he's had trouble finding scoring 5-on-5, so we challenge him all the time to get the puck back and not wait until it comes to him. He's like a lot of guys. If he gets the puck back, he's better with it."

ZACH #8 WERENSKI

20, D, DRAFTED 1ST ROUND, 8TH OVERALL, IN 2015

BY AARON PORTZLINE

Zach Werenski was only five years old, so some of the memories are pretty blurry. But there are vivid snapshots still fresh in his mind.

In June 2002, Zach's parents drove him and his older brother, Brad, to downtown Detroit, where more than one million fans gathered to witness the Detroit Red Wings' third Stanley Cup parade in six seasons. "I remember being there with all of the people, and I remember the Red Wings coming by with the Cup," Zach said. "I remember seeing all the Red Wings players waving to the crowd."

But something else happened that day to the future Columbus Blue Jackets' standout defenseman. "After that, I knew what I really wanted to do in life," Zach said. "I wanted to play in the NHL. It definitely helps, when you're a young kid, to see something like that."

Soon Zach was learning how to skate and playing youth hockey near his home in Lake St. Clair, a suburb of Detroit. He collected posters of his favorite players and covered his bedroom walls with Red Wings' players like Steve Yzerman, Kirk Maltby and, of course, Nicklas Lidstrom, one of the best defensemen in NHL history.

With so many former Red Wings staying around Detroit after they retired as players,

Zach had great coaches who taught him how to play like the Red Wings play – as a unit of five, emphasizing puck possession and hammering home the mantra "share the puck, share the glory."

> ## "IT'S NO FUN GOING TO THE RINK IF YOU DON'T LOVE IT, AND IF YOU DON'T LOVE IT, YOU'LL NEVER MAKE IT TO THE NHL."
> ### ZACH WERENSKI

He also learned a really important skill for defensemen: rather than look down to see the puck on his stick, Zach is constantly looking up, surveying the ice and the position of players in front of him. "I've been told many times that I was taught the right way," he said.

Zach credits his parents, Ken and Kristen, with not letting his passion become an

obsession. Hockey was a big part of his life, and playing in the NHL was always his goal. He ate healthy food, worked out regularly and watched hockey religiously, especially the Stanley Cup playoffs. But hockey was never the most important part of his life. "I didn't ever really get too serious with it," Zach said. "I was on the ice pretty much year-round, but I did it for fun in the summer. You hear a lot about nightmare hockey parents, and I know they're out there… But my parents weren't like that at all. I never played on select teams. I never travelled in the summer for hockey. I played lacrosse. I golfed a ton and hung out with my friends in the summer."

When he was 12 years old, Zach was at a family party during the summer months. He was planning to leave early with his father so he could go to tryouts for a nearby select travel team. "But I didn't want to leave the party and neither did my dad," Zach said. "So we didn't go. I'm really close with family and aunts and uncles and cousins, so whenever I can have time with them, it's special."

By taking a break each off-season, Zach fed his passion when the weather turned cool. He never suffered burnout like some kids his age. "When the season started, I wanted to be there," Zach said. "I wanted to

2016-17 STATS   GP 78 | G 11 | A 36 | PTS 47 | PIM 14

"MY FAVORITE PLAYER GROWING UP WAS SIDNEY CROSBY...THE FIRST TIME I LINED UP AGAINST HIM WAS INCREDIBLE."

ZACH WERENSKI

work hard at the rink. It's no fun going to the rink if you don't love it, and if you don't love it, you'll never make it to the NHL."

Zach became more serious about hockey in 2013 when he went to play for the U.S. National Team Development Program in nearby Ann Arbor, Mich., when he was 16 years old. At that point, it was a quick trip to the NHL. He played one season (2015-16) at the University of Michigan, then made the leap to pro hockey – the American Hockey League – to end the season.

Zach was a standout in the AHL, winning the Calder Cup with the Lake Erie Monsters in 2016. It was his play in the AHL that convinced the Blue Jackets, including coach John Tortorella, that he was ready to play at the highest level.

Zach had an amazing rookie season in the NHL, totalling 11 goals and 36 assists for 47 points. His superb season made him a finalist for the Calder Trophy, the NHL's rookie of the year award, along with the Winnipeg Jets' Patrik Laine and the Toronto Maple Leafs' Auston Matthews, who won the award.

What was the coolest part of his rookie season? "Lining up against your favorite players as a kid, that's one of the coolest things," Zach said. "For me, my favorite player growing up was Sidney Crosby. I wanted to be him. The first time I lined up against him, I thought that was incredible. It didn't go too well. He scored the second shift I was out there, but we ended up winning the game, so it was fine."

Playing his first game in Detroit was exciting, too. On Dec. 9, Zach had a whole throng of friends and family sitting near the glass in Joe Louis Arena when the Blue Jackets visited the Red Wings. "My parents, my parents' friends and bunch of my friends were all there," Zach said. "In warmups I got a couple of selfies with them. It was pretty wild. I grew up watching the Wings. I was on the other side of the glass last year, but now I'm on the ice."

MITCH #16
MARNER

TORONTO MAPLE LEAFS

20, RW, DRAFTED 1ST ROUND,
4TH OVERALL, IN 2015

BY KEN CAMPBELL

There was a time when Mitch Marner and Connor McDavid regularly went head-to-head, both beacons for their teams despite playing with players a year older. The last time they met before junior hockey was in the all-Ontario championship. Marner's team won 4-2. Marner had four points and McDavid had two.

McDavid was always bigger and stronger than Marner, though not always better. Sometimes Marner was the best player in a tournament and McDavid was the second best, and just as many times it was the other way around. Because he was so small, Marner went back down to his age group after that season and dominated the competition. McDavid continued to play beyond his years and dominated as well. It was about that time the McDavid legend began to grow. Marner, meanwhile, wasn't growing a whole lot at all.

It still rankles his father, Paul, a little bit. He recalls a night during the 2015 OHL playoffs (March 31) when McDavid had one assist in an overtime win over the Sarnia Sting that made all the highlight shows. The same night, the London Knights went into Kitchener and beat the Rangers 10-6. Marner had six points. Not a mention. "I tell people all the time, the Connor McDavid

effect for my kid has been the biggest shadow you could cast," Paul said. "What Mitch did in the OHL statistically, people would

> ## "I DON'T KNOW IF I EXPECTED TO DO WHAT I'M DOING RIGHT NOW, BUT IT'S REALLY FUN AND I THINK IT'S GOING TO KEEP GETTING BETTER."
> **MITCH MARNER**

have normally been drooling over him as a first-overall pick. He put up 126 points that year, and his numbers were crazy. But because Connor was in that draft, it just didn't matter."

The Oilers took McDavid with the No. 1 pick, and nobody with any hockey intelligence would suggest they picked the wrong player. But the Maple Leafs were able to get Marner fourth overall because he was the

little guy who had done nothing but shut the mouths of his critics at every turn. And he continues to do so. The sublime puck skills, the incredible vision, the footwork, the ability to hang onto the puck that he demonstrated in junior are almost as dominant now that they're on display in the NHL. And the funny thing is Marner isn't that small. He's creeping in on six feet, and listed (albeit generously) at 170 pounds, and his father believes there's room to grow, both literally and figuratively. "He's still growing now, and I believe he'll be about 6-foot-1," Paul said. "My older guy kept growing until he was 22 or 23, and he's 6-foot-2 now. A lot of the kids there now have hit their physical peaks and have been for a couple of years, but I think Mitch has another 20 pounds and maybe an inch or two to go still."

As an 18-year-old in the OHL in 2015-16, Marner was named regular season MVP, playoff MVP, Memorial Cup MVP and CHL Player of the Year. The only other player to accomplish that feat in the history of junior hockey is Brad Richards. Yet even after that, questions remained about whether or not Marner would be able to play in the NHL as a 19-year-old. They were legitimate questions, as silly and misguided as they look now. "I don't know if I expected to do

---

2016-17 STATS   GP 77 | G 19 | A 42 | PTS 61 | PIM 38

what I'm doing right now, but it's really fun and I think it's going to keep getting better," Marner said. "It's really helped a lot playing with 'JVR' (James van Riemsdyk) and 'Bozie' (Tyler Bozak). They've been a big help to me."

Those who have watched the Leafs would beg to differ. In reality, Marner has quite often been carrying that line with his vision and passing, much the way he did with Max Domi and Christian Dvorak in London. Near the mid-season mark of 2016-17, Marner had 10 goals and 32 points in 39 games, the Leafs were on the cusp of a playoff spot and van Riemsdyk was one of their hottest players with a goal and nine points in five games. Six of those points came on goals that were either scored or assisted by Marner.

In another year, Marner might win the Calder Trophy. This season, however, he's not even the best rookie on his own team. He wasn't even among the finalists when Auston Matthews took home the Calder in June. But the Leafs know what they have in Marner. Assistant GM Mark Hunter has known it since he had him in London, and scout Lindsay Hofford has known it since he had him on a spring hockey team when he was eight years old. "He's a proud kid," Paul said. "At every level he's ever been at, he's always been the best player or one of the best players."

It will be a tall order for Marner to match that at the NHL level, but it would be foolhardy to underestimate him.

IVAN #9 PROVOROV

20, D, DRAFTED 1ST ROUND, 7TH OVERALL, IN 2015

BY WAYNE FISH

Imagine being just 13 years old and leaving home to become a stranger in a strange land. Saying goodbye to family, friends and, yes, even all your favorite food. Stepping on a big jet airplane, flying halfway around Planet Earth, just to chase a dream.

It sounds like the fantasy of many young players who can only dream of playing in the NHL. For a young Ivan Provorov, however, it was terrifying, it was demanding, though most of all, it was fun.

Seven years ago, Ivan and his family decided the best way for him to make it to the NHL was to pack his bags and leave his native Russia for North America. This meant he was going to have to learn a whole new language, pick up foreign customs and make new friends.

At first, it wasn't easy. He needed some time to acclimate to his surroundings in Cedar Rapids, Iowa, playing for the Rough-Riders of the United States Hockey League. But everyone was friendly and quickly he mastered the language, the culture and, perhaps most importantly, how to eat pizza. "It was hard not being able to see my family," Ivan said. "But it's a sacrifice I had to make to get to where I am now."

Even before his 14th birthday, his whole purpose was consumed with the idea of be-

ing the best he could be. "From Day 1, that was my goal," Ivan said. "Ever since I started playing hockey, I wanted to play in the NHL. My parents and I thought coming to North America was the best way to go and get better…to learn the culture, the language, get used to the ice. I had a lot of sacrifices to make for myself and my family, but they paid off. I was willing to do everything to make the NHL."

Within two years, he was off to Canada to play junior hockey for the Brandon Wheat Kings of the Western Hockey League. Then in 2015, the Flyers made him their first draft pick. Just over a year later, he surprised everyone by making the Flyers' roster as a 19-year-old.

Ivan would go on to enjoy a stellar season, becoming the first rookie in Flyers franchise history to lead the team in ice time, averaging more than 21 minutes per game. And to think, it all started back in Yaroslavl, Russia, when he was just a little tyke. "The first time I watched hockey on TV, I was about four," he said. "I got my skates for my fifth birthday. That's how it started."

At first, he didn't know what position he was going to play. "The first couple years, you really don't have a position," Ivan said. "When I turned about nine, I started to play

defense."

Ivan's favorite pro player growing up was former Detroit defenseman Nicklas

> ## "I HAD A LOT OF SACRIFICES TO MAKE FOR MYSELF AND MY FAMILY, BUT THEY PAID OFF. I WAS WILLING TO DO EVERYTHING TO MAKE THE NHL."
> ### IVAN PROVOROV

Lidstrom, the all-purpose blueliner who was inducted into Hall of Fame just a couple years back.

If being able to play like Lidstrom required more effort than usual, Ivan was willing to make the sacrifice.

Things like perfecting the art of skating backward were important. "Yes, I always took extra skating lessons," he said. "I really focused on skating."

2016-17 STATS GP **82** | G **6** | A **24** | PTS **30** | PIM **34**

"MY PARENTS HELPED ME
WITH A LOT OF STUFF. MY DAD MOSTLY
WITH HOCKEY, MY MOM WITH
HELPING ME WITH SCHOOL."

IVAN PROVOROV

If you watch Ivan's game today, you can see some of the elements that Lidstrom perfected. "I liked just how well-rounded he was," Ivan said. "He was one of the best two-way defensemen. He played a lot, did everything he could to help the team win."

The quest for Ivan culminated on the final day of the Flyers' 2016 training camp. He was sitting at his dressing room stall when coach Dave Hakstol approached and told him he had made the team.

Ivan picked up his cell phone and called home, where it was 4 a.m. His dad, Vladimir (who runs a construction company), answered. Ivan told him what had just happened. There was shouting and screaming throughout the Provorov household. Vladimir was so excited he couldn't go back to sleep.

Ivan knows he couldn't have gotten this far without the support of his dad and mom (Venera, who is a cardiologist), plus his sister, Alexandra, and younger brother, Vladimir, who is nine. "My dad, even though he never played hockey, he's got the smarts and everything," Ivan said. "He understands hockey better than anybody. When I have a chance, I tell him all the small details (of his play with the Flyers)."

Even now, Ivan calls home frequently because that is still where the foundation of his life exists. "My parents helped me with a lot of stuff," he said. "My dad mostly with the hockey, my mom with helping me with school. Got help from both sides. I can't thank them enough."

If Ivan were to coach a bunch of nine-year-olds like Vladimir, what would he tell them? "Get low on your skates, keep your head up," he said. "Don't look at the puck and stuff like that. Work hard, have fun, enjoy it."

Who knows? The next Ivan Provorov might be reading this and wondering if the dream, for him, is possible. No one will know, of course, unless he tries like Ivan did.

SEBASTIAN #20
AHO

20, RW, DRAFTED 2ND ROUND, 35TH OVERALL, IN 2015

BY LUKE DECOCK

Sebastian Aho was just two years old the first time he put on skates and got on the ice. Even then, he went straight for the net, just like he does now in the NHL, or at least he tried. "With a little help, he managed to do that," said his father, Harri. "It took a while though."

Growing up in Finland, Sebastian spent his entire life around hockey. His father played for Karpat Oulu, his hometown team, before becoming the team's general manager. When Sebastian was a little kid, he took his father's equipment and told him he'd be playing with him in a couple of years. It took a little longer than that.

Sebastian was only 17 when he made Karpat's professional roster, playing against men twice his age. In the fall of 2016, at 19, he came over to North America to play for the Carolina Hurricanes. He ended up with 24 goals and 49 points, second on his team and fifth among rookies in the NHL.

He spent his childhood hanging out in the Karpat dressing room and going to games to watch his father play, and he expected to do the same when he grew up. He always thought he would be a hockey player like his father. He turned out to be an even better one. "I grew up in hockey," Sebastian said. "I was in his locker room when I was just a

baby. I saw it so close – what it's like to be a professional hockey player. It's always been my No. 1 thing, to be a hockey player."

As important as hockey was to Sebastian growing up, it wasn't the only sport he played. With his older brother and other

> ## "I GREW UP IN HOCKEY. I WAS IN MY FATHER'S LOCKER ROOM WHEN I WAS JUST A BABY. I SAW IT SO CLOSE – WHAT IT'S LIKE TO BE A PROFESSIONAL HOCKEY PLAYER."
>
> ### SEBASTIAN AHO

kids in his neighborhood, they'd play just about anything when they were outside, soccer and everything else. "I was a pretty curious guy, asking a lot of questions, pretty

happy," Sebastian said. "I liked to play every ball game a lot. It didn't matter which sport, I just played. I was in a neighborhood with lots of same-age guys, and we played pretty much everything."

But from that first day he put on skates, Sebastian loved playing hockey. He started playing for a team at three years old, and it was always his first love and favorite sport. His father would bring his teammates' sticks home from the rink, and instead of saving them as souvenirs, Sebastian and his older brother Samuli would play with them until they broke. Playing against Samuli, who is three years older, taught Sebastian how to play against bigger players. Even now, at 5-foot-11, 172 pounds, Sebastian is smaller than most of the other players he sees in the NHL.

By the time he was 13, he was playing against kids four and five years older than him. They were bigger and stronger and faster, but Sebastian had skill and learned to be tricky on the ice. His father could see he was going to be a hockey player, but he had no idea how good he was going to turn out to be. "I knew, when he was about 12 years old, that he will be a pro hockey player," Harri said. "Not until last year did I begin to think NHL. Dreams are dreams, but daily

2016-17 STATS   GP 82 | G 24 | A 25 | PTS 49 | PIM 26

"HE OBSERVED EVERYTHING AND DIDN'T MISS ANYTHING WHILE VISITING THE LOCKER ROOM AND THE GAMES."

HARRI AHO, SEBASTIAN'S FATHER

work counts – you are only as good as your last shift. I knew all the time how important it is to be ready when you get the chance to play in NHL."

In Sebastian's last season in Finland, he took home bronze in the Finnish League with Karpat (after winning the championship in 2015), won a gold medal at the world juniors with Finland and a silver at the World Championship in Russia playing against NHL players. He knew it was time to play in the NHL.

Moving to a foreign country wasn't easy. In his first few weeks in the United States, he lived at the house of teammate and fellow Finnish forward Teuvo Teravainen while Sebastian worked on speaking English. Still, it didn't take Sebastian long to adjust to the NHL. Even though he didn't score his first goal until the 14th game of the season, once he started scoring, he scored a lot – 24 in the final 69 games. It wasn't just his offense, though.

From the start of the season, even when Sebastian wasn't scoring, Hurricanes coach Bill Peters liked how he played defense and worked hard at both ends of the ice. That was nothing new for Sebastian's father, who saw him doing that as a young boy. Even in the NHL, that hasn't changed. "First of all, he got his values from home, and his passion for hockey turned on at a very early age," Harri said. "He had a chance to come to the locker room when I played. He really admired the players and wanted to become like them one day. He observed everything and didn't miss anything while visiting the locker room and the games. Of course, he had the talent for hockey, but the commitment and the work ethic are the key points that I have taught him."

Sebastian may have been born to play hockey, but he still had to work his way to the NHL, where his rookie season was just the beginning for him.

ANTHONY #39 MANTHA

23, RW, DRAFTED FIRST ROUND, 20TH OVERALL, IN 2013

BY BOB DUFF

For Anthony Mantha, it was like he'd come full circle in his hockey life. Here he was, an NHL rookie, once again skating outdoors, feeling the cool wind blow through his hair at BMO Field on New Year's Day, 2017, as his Detroit Red Wings battled the Toronto Maple Leafs.

Anthony scored twice, including the tying goal with 1.1 seconds left to play. What a day to remember. And remember Anthony did.

That winter afternoon brought him right back home to the Montreal suburb of Longueuil, where Anthony grew up and where he fell in love with hockey while skating on the open ice of the neighborhood pond. "It all comes down to the outdoor rink, with dad, grandpa, sisters and friends," Anthony said. "I lived probably a two-minute walking distance from a nice little pond. We would bring our net and stay on there for hours."

Anthony, his sisters Kim, Elizabeth and Barbara, his dad Daniel and especially his grandfather Andre Pronovost would lace up their skates, grab their sticks and set out chasing that puck. Anthony was three years old when he first learned to skate, but soon hockey was a big part of his young life. "When I was maybe seven or eight, I remember playing summer hockey," Anthony said. "We'd always go to some big

tournaments, in big cities like Boston or Toronto. That was far when you are a little kid, and you'd just have so much fun. It's good memories."

For as far back as he can remember, Anthony thought of nothing other than being in the NHL. "I actually always wanted to be

> ## "IN FOURTH GRADE, WE HAD TO DO A FUTURE PROJECT... I WROTE THAT I WANTED TO BE A PRO HOCKEY PLAYER."
> ### ANTHONY MANTHA

a hockey player," Anthony said. "In fourth grade, we had to do a future project. When you're a kid, you just kind of scribble on the page, but I wrote that I wanted to be a pro hockey player."

His dream came true, and sometimes, Anthony wonders how many of the other kids were as lucky as him and got to live out

their childhood dream. "Who knows?" he said. "Maybe there are a couple of other kids who went on to do exactly what they wrote, but it usually doesn't happen that way."

It happened that way for him, and he couldn't be happier about it. Of course, Anthony will be the first to admit that he was offered a bit of an advantage when it came to understanding what he was going to need to do in order to earn a career in the NHL.

You see, his grandfather – Pronovost, the man who would skate with young Anthony on the pond – was a legend in Montreal.

From 1956 to 1960, the Montreal Canadiens won the Stanley Cup five years in a row. No other NHL franchise has ever done that, and Anthony's grandfather played on the last four of those teams.

Pronovost, a left winger, scored 16 goals for the 1957-58 Canadiens, one fewer than Anthony scored for the Red Wings during the 2016-17 season.

The men Anthony's grandfather played alongside, the men who came to the house to visit and spend time with Anthony and his grandfather, were living legends – Jean Beliveau, Dickie Moore, Boom-Boom Geoffrion and, of course, the captain of those outstanding Montreal teams, Maurice

2016-17 STATS GP 60 | G 17 | A 19 | PTS 36 | PIM 53

"I THINK ANTHONY MANTHA IS GOING TO BE A REALLY GOOD PLAYER IN THIS LEAGUE AND COULD BE A GREAT PLAYER IN THIS LEAGUE."

JEFF BLASHILL, DETROIT RED WINGS COACH

Richard, the first player in NHL history to score 50 goals in a season.

Anthony never saw any of these great men play the game, but he knew of their exploits - partly due to his grandfather, and partly because when you grow up in Montreal, you learn everything there is to know about the great tradition of the Canadiens. "Being a French-Canadian, your idol is Maurice Richard," Anthony said. "He's probably one of the best players that played hockey. That my grandpa played with him, you know, it's something he'd tell me stories about."

Anthony's grandfather would take him to the Habs games, fuelling his love for the game even more. "When I was younger, he brought me to the rink, brought me skating," Anthony said. "From around the age of eight or nine to 15 or 16, he told me to just have fun. Those are the years that you need to have fun. Once I started playing junior, he was more talking to me about what I needed to do, probably more of this and that. He knew what the scouts were looking for. We would talk on how to get my game better. He's just been great for me through-out the years."

Detroit drafted him 20th overall in 2013. With the Val-d'Or Foreuers of the QMJHL in 2013-14, Anthony led all of the CHL in scoring with 57 goals and 63 assists. Anthony got his first chance in the NHL with the Red Wings in 2015-16, scoring two goals in 10 games. He made it as a regular in 2016-17, and his 17 goals were tied for third on the team. "I think Anthony Mantha is going to be a really good player in this league and could be a great player in this league," said Detroit coach Jeff Blashill.

If and when he does, Anthony will never forget those days skating on the pond with his family, because they continue. "Still to this day, every Christmas, both families – my mom's and my dad's – meet up and we play hockey, a little pickup game," Anthony said.

You can take the kid from the neighbor-hood pond to the big pond, but no matter how far he goes or how big he makes it, you'll never take the kid out of him.

MATTHEW #19 TKACHUK

19, LW, DRAFTED 1ST ROUND, 6TH OVERALL, IN 2016

BY RANDY SPORTAK

Matthew Tkachuk's father is considered one of the best American-born hockey players in NHL history. Keith Tkachuk collected more than 500 goals and 1,000 points over his 18 seasons in the league, plus represented the United States at four Winter Olympics and two World Cup of Hockey tournaments while being one of the game's premier power forwards.

With such a successful star for a dad, you would think it'd mean all hockey all the time for Matthew as a youngster, but that wasn't the case for the Calgary Flames left winger. Sure, Matthew was playing hockey as soon as he could lace up skates and hold a stick, but his sporting interests were never held to just one activity.

Pick a game, any game, and odds are Matthew played it, often with the same rambunctious unbridled enthusiasm he used to become one of the top rookies in the NHL in 2016-17.

Although he was born in Scottsdale, Ariz., where his father played for the Coyotes, the Tkachuk family moved to St. Louis when Matthew was five, after Keith was traded to the Blues, so naturally he played baseball during the summer in the city where Major League Baseball's St. Louis Cardinals are king.

But his sporting choices didn't end there. Matthew was a goalie in soccer throughout his elementary school years. During his middle school years, he played as many sports as possible, including lacrosse, basketball and football, plus being active playing golf and swimming with friends. "I know now kids play hockey all year round,"

> ## "I THINK IT'S SO IMPORTANT FOR KIDS TO PLAY AS MANY SPORTS AS THEY CAN."
> ### MATTHEW TKACHUK

Matthew said. "In summer, kids work with skills coaches and skating coaches – I believe in those – but I think it's so important for kids to play as many sports as they can. It's different for each person, and if they're going to be a pro athlete they have to pick one over the other, but until a couple years

ago, I didn't start playing hockey until a couple weeks before the season started. It never occurred to me how you'd have to pick one sport. Those friends I had when I was younger are my closest friends now."

Matthew was finally forced to concentrate solely on hockey in the fall of 2013 when he joined the U.S. National Team Development Program and skated on the Under-17 team.

After years of excelling in the St. Louis AAA Blues program, he moved to Michigan for the NTDP for a couple glorious seasons, which included gold medal victories at the World U-17 Hockey Challenge in his first year and the U-18 World Championship in his second season on a team that featured Toronto Maple Leafs star Auston Matthews. Even at that age, it appeared to be a certainty Matthew was destined to be in the NHL. "His personality, just his stubbornness to get to where he wanted to be – that made me know he was going to be in the NHL," said his former NTDP linemate and close friend Jack Roslovic, a first-round pick of the Winnipeg Jets in 2015. "Not only did he have that, but he had that swagger and belief he'd be a good player."

Maybe it was his stubbornness or perhaps it was simply being practical, but after his two seasons with the development team

2016-17 STATS   GP 76 | G 13 | A 35 | PTS 48 | PIM 105

> ## "HIS PERSONALITY, JUST HIS STUBBORNNESS TO GET TO WHERE HE WANTED TO BE – THAT MADE ME KNOW HE WAS GOING TO BE IN THE NHL."
>
> **JACK ROSLOVIC, MATTHEW'S FORMER NTDP LINEMATE AND CLOSE FRIEND**

Matthew took a detour from the expected path by choosing to play for the London Knights of the Ontario Hockey League instead of following the route his father took, playing college hockey. His dad played one season at Boston University, where Tkachuk's younger brother, Brady, an expected top-10 draft pick in 2018, is slated to go in the fall. ("It'd be really cool if he got drafted by Calgary," Matthew said.) But Matthew decided he'd take the major junior route.

The combination of a busier game schedule compared to college hockey's, combined with the professional-caliber coaching staff and program instilled by Knights' coach, president and owner Dale Hunter was worth pursuing. "I believed that was the path that would take me the fastest to the NHL and really prepare me for it," said Matthew, whose trademark look while playing is chomping on his mouthguard. "I'll never know if the other way was better for me, but I think it was the right decision."

You certainly can't disagree with Tkachuk on that assessment. After being drafted by the Flames last year, he had an immediate impact while helping the team make it back to the playoffs. He scored 13 goals and collected 48 points in the regular season and created plenty of much-needed energy, emotion and moxie for the club with his crash-and-bang style.

Certainly opposing players were forced to take notice. "He did a really good job of establishing himself in the league," Roslovic said. "The way he acts on the ice, kind of like the bully, he doesn't do off the ice. So I think that's where his anger goes."

JAKOB #6 CHYCHRUN

19, D, DRAFTED 1ST ROUND, 16TH OVERALL, IN 2016

BY SARAH MCLELLAN

Growing up in Florida, Jakob Chychrun was outside every single day playing sports with the kids in his neighborhood. But they weren't lining up for a hockey game. They were shooting basketballs and throwing footballs. "I really enjoyed being an athlete," Jakob said. "I enjoyed competing in other sports."

Jakob also played baseball, soccer, tennis and golf. His dad, Jeff, encouraged him to try other activities, and Jakob did, finding out he had plenty of interests besides hockey.

Still, that was the sport Jakob knew he wanted to stick with and what he wanted do for a living. And Jakob has made that dream come true, breaking into the NHL as an 18-year-old defenseman with the Arizona Coyotes. "I knew at a pretty young age that this is what I could do with my life, what I wanted to do," he said.

Falling in love with hockey wasn't unusual for Jakob.

His dad played in the NHL for parts of eight seasons, skating for the Flyers, Kings, Penguins and Oilers in the 1980s and '90s before retiring and settling in Florida, and Jakob was introduced to the sport early in life. He was in skates at the age of two and attended Panthers games. His first organized skates were with the Panthers' mascot, and

he joined a team when he was four. By the time he was six years old, Jakob was traveling all over Florida to compete. "The feeling I'd have when I was playing, there's nothing like it," he said. "When you're passionate about something, there's really no other option. There shouldn't be any other option other than to follow what you love and to chase your goals. I was really dedicated at a young age and really wanted to try to be the best, one day. So I think at a young age, I was just able to work toward that. I'm lucky I knew what I wanted to do at such a young age."

When he was 13, Jakob began playing with a team in Michigan, but his family didn't move from Boca Raton, Florida. Instead, Jakob flew to Detroit on Thursdays or Fridays to meet up with his team for the weekend. "I had to really be disciplined and have good time management with getting school work done on the planes and studying for tests on the way back," he said. "It was tough, but it definitely taught me a lot of life lessons."

Eventually, Jakob left Florida for Toronto to play one season of midget hockey. In 2014-15, he started with the Sarnia Sting after they took him first overall in the Ontario Hockey League draft.

In his first season with the Sting, Jakob thrived. He scored 16 goals, finished with 33 points in 42 games and was nominated for outstanding rookie, top defenseman and player of the year.

> ## "I KNEW AT A PRETTY YOUNG AGE THAT THIS IS WHAT I COULD DO WITH MY LIFE, WHAT I WANTED TO DO."
>
> **JAKOB CHYCHRUN**

But he was playing with a tear in his left shoulder and had to undergo surgery to fix the injury. He was off the ice for three months but was cleared to return for the start of the next season.

He remained a key player for Sarnia, racking up 49 points in 62 games. But he felt he could have had a bigger impact on the Sting if he had more time to train in the off-season.

2016-17 STATS GP 68 | G 7 | A 13 | PTS 20 | PIM 47

"I WAS REALLY DEDICATED AT A YOUNG AGE AND REALLY WANTED TO TRY TO BE THE BEST, ONE DAY."

JAKOB CHYCHRUN

Still, Jakob was ranked the fourth-best skater in North America by NHL Central Scouting.

Although some projected him to be at the top of the 2016 class, Jakob wasn't drafted among the first 10 picks. But he did go in the first round, getting taken 16th overall by the Coyotes after they made a trade with the Red Wings to move up in the draft order.

Jakob expected to make the NHL right away as an 18-year-old, and he did. He impressed the Coyotes at training camp with his poise on the blueline as a smart, skilled and smooth-skating puck-moving defenseman. He earned a roster spot and made his NHL debut on Oct.15, 2016, against the Flyers in Arizona. "It's what I expected to do," Jakob said. "It's what I wanted to do. I wanted to achieve what I had in mind for myself."

In just his second game, Jakob scored his first career NHL goal against the Canadiens in Montreal. He became the first rookie defenseman in franchise history to record a point in his first three games. In total, Jakob finished with 20 points in 68 games. His seven goals were tied for the second-most among rookie defensemen in 2016-17. "I knew it was something I would be able to handle and be able to do," he said. "I would have felt like it would have been tough to go back to junior this year. I just feel like I was ready for this next step."

Getting to the NHL required focus, determination and sacrifice, especially when Jakob lived in Florida while playing in Michigan. "I didn't really have a weekend ever for, like, two years," he said. "I couldn't really do many things that a regular kid would do, like just hang out with their buddies."

But Jakob doesn't regret the decisions he made because he was able to turn his dream into a reality. He made it to the NHL. "It's exciting times ahead," he said. "Now it's just a matter of continuing to improve on every year you play and continue to get better year by year."

FABULOUS FRESHMEN

HERE'S A SNEAK PEEK AT THE ROOKIES WHO'LL BE MAKING HEADLINES IN 2017-18

Fantastic rookies have been all the rage in recent years as the average age in the NHL continues to decline. It's no wonder why, though, with the quality crop of talent that has sprouted up.

Take Connor McDavid, for example. The Edmonton Oilers all-star topped the league as the only 100-point scorer in 2016-17 in just his second season. Meanwhile, in Toronto, the Maple Leafs were led back to the post-season by the amazing Auston Matthews, who battled in the rookie scoring race with sharpshooting sniper Patrik Laine.

BY JARED CLINTON

THERE MAY BE NO MCDAVID, MATTHEWS OR LAINE ENTERING THE LEAGUE IN 2017-18, BUT IT IS SURE TO HAVE ITS FILL OF REMARKABLE ROOKIES:

CLAYTON KELLER
ARIZONA COYOTES
DRAFTED 1ST ROUND (7TH OVERALL) IN 2016
19, C/LW, 5-FOOT-10, 168 LBS.

Good things come in small packages, and Keller is proof of that. His 5-foot-10 frame may not strike fear into the hearts of defenders, but his speed and skill with the puck certainly does. Arizona has a great group of prospects, but Keller is the brightest of the bunch.

NOLAN PATRICK
PHILADELPHIA FLYERS
DRAFTED 1ST ROUND (2ND OVERALL) IN 2017
19, C/RW, 6-FOOT-3, 198 LBS.

The term "generational player" hasn't been thrown around when talking about Patrick, but the smooth-skating two-way center has all the tools to become a top-line star in Philly. He's whip-smart and wickedly creative, and his brain for the game could see him turning in a Calder-caliber campaign.

BROCK BOESER
VANCOUVER CANUCKS
DRAFTED 1ST ROUND (23RD OVERALL) IN 2015
20, RW, 6-FOOT-1, 192 LBS.

His short stint with the Canucks in 2016-17 was an appetizer for 2017-18's main course. Boeser can snap a shot off in the blink of an eye and his playmaking ability is the cherry on top of his skill set. Skating with the Sedins could make him Vancouver's greatest goal scorer.

CHARLIE MCAVOY
BOSTON BRUINS
DRAFTED 1ST ROUND (14TH OVERALL) IN 2016
19, D, 6-FOOT-1, 212 LBS.

McAvoy made the move from the NCAA to the NHL playoffs look like a breeze as he took on a top-pairing role in an instant. He can run the power play, shutdown an attack and produce points at a big-league rate. He's ready to be a big-time blueliner for the Bruins.

TYSON JOST
COLORADO AVALANCHE
DRAFTED 1ST ROUND (10TH OVERALL) IN 2016
19, C/LW, 5-FOOT-11, 194 LBS.

Jost has tried to model his game after Jonathan Toews, and the Avalanche would be very happy if Jost can help Colorado climb the mountain the same way the Chicago captain has helped the Blackhawks. Jost's speed and versatility makes him a perfect cornerstone player for the rebuilding Avalanche.

MATHEW BARZAL
NEW YORK ISLANDERS
DRAFTED 1ST ROUND (16TH OVERALL) IN 2015
20, C, 6-FOOT, 187 LBS.

A pass-first player with hawk-like vision and more offensive imagination than he knows what to do with, Barzal is coming along at just the right time. The Islanders are looking to beef up their power play, and Barzal could become the setup man New York has always wanted for John Tavares.

DYLAN STROME
ARIZONA COYOTES
DRAFTED 1ST ROUND (3RD OVERALL) IN 2015
20, C, 6-FOOT-3, 198 LBS.

He's not the swiftest skater, but Strome could find the scoresheet if it was a needle in a haystack on a pitch-black night. He's a point-producing machine and few have torn up the major junior ranks the way he has. He's one to watch on the up-and-coming Coyotes.

JOSHUA HO-SANG
NEW YORK ISLANDERS
DRAFTED 1ST ROUND (28TH OVERALL) IN 2014
21, C/RW, 6-FOOT, 172 LBS.

Watching Ho-Sang play with the puck is a treat, and dangerous dekes are the name of his game. He has hands softer than the finest silk and the ability to make a defenseman's head spin and ankles buckle. There's no rookie with as much raw talent as Ho-Sang.

NICO HISCHIER
NEW JERSEY DEVILS
DRAFTED 1ST ROUND (1ST OVERALL) IN 2017
18, C, 6-FOOT, 179 LBS.

Creativity can be the key to offensive success, and Hischier has shown a knack for on-ice artistry. Don't take that to mean he can't rely on brute force, though. The Swiss sniper owns a booming shot. Given the space, he can blister a blast past even the best netminders.

JOEL ERIKSSON EK
MINNESOTA WILD
DRAFTED 1ST ROUND (20TH OVERALL) IN 2015
20, C/LW, 6-FOOT-2, 203 LBS.

Eriksson Ek has the shot and smarts to make something happen every time he's on the ice, and he's ready to make his presence felt in the State of Hockey. Standing 6-foot-2 and 200 pounds, he is ready for the rough and tumble Western Conference.

MS

SO YOU THINK YOU KNOW THE NHL,
DO YOU? TEST YOUR KNOWLEDGE
OF THE LEAGUE'S 30 TEAMS FROM
THE 2016-17 SEASON AS WELL AS
IT'S NEWEST ADDITION: THE VEGAS
GOLDEN KNIGHTS

COREY PERRY #10

ANAHEIM DUCKS

UNDER COACH BRUCE BOUDREAU, THE Anaheim Ducks were the best team in the Pacific, quacking their way to the division title every year and racking up more points than any other team in the league from 2012-13 to 2015-16. Yet despite being only a short drive from Disneyland, Anaheim wasn't the happiest place on earth when the playoffs came around. The Ducks didn't get to lift the Stanley Cup once under Boudreau, and that meant changes had to be made.

Two days after the Ducks were knocked out of the playoffs in 2016, Boudreau was fired and Anaheim made what was old new again behind the bench. Randy Carlyle, who helped the Ducks win the franchise's only Stanley Cup in 2007, was named the new coach.

As always, the Ducks were led by their star dynamic duo of Ryan Getzlaf and Corey Perry in 2016-17, and it was a record-setting year for Getzlaf. Less than one month into the season, the Ducks' captain passed Hall of Famer Teemu Selanne to become the franchise's all-time leader in assists with a whopping 532. When the season was over, Getzlaf had 578 career assists, a total only 94 other players have achieved in NHL history.

The veteran Ducks were joined by some star ducklings, too. Rickard Rakell used his lightning-fast shot to become one of the league's top goal scorers, and Cam Fowler spread his wings to become the best defenseman in Anaheim's lineup. Meanwhile, opposing teams needed a magnifying glass to find a hole in young goaltender John Gibson. He was so good, in fact, that he was sent to the All-Star Game to represent the team.

It was no surprise that Anaheim won the Pacific Division for the fifth-straight season, piling up more than 100 points for the fourth year in a row. It seems that Carlyle's return to Anaheim has put the Ducks on the road to becoming mighty once again.

LEADERS

POINTS
RYAN GETZLAF
73

GOALS
RICKARD RAKELL
33

ASSISTS
RYAN GETZLAF
58

PENALTY MINUTES
JARED BOLL
87

ICE TIME
CAM FOWLER
24:50

GOALS-AGAINST AVERAGE
JOHN GIBSON
2.22

SAVE PERCENTAGE
JOHN GIBSON
.924

PRESIDENT MICHAEL SCHULMAN
GENERAL MANAGER BOB MURRAY
COACH RANDY CARLYLE
MASCOT WILD WING

RECORD
46-23-13

HOME
29-8-4

AWAY
17-15-9

POINTS
105

GOALS FOR
220

GOALS AGAINST
197

AVERAGE AGE
27.6

ROOKIES
4

TOP PROSPECT
JACOB LARSON
D, 19,
ACQUIRED:
2014 DRAFT,
27TH OVERALL

HOME JERSEY

DRAW
YOUR OWN
MASK

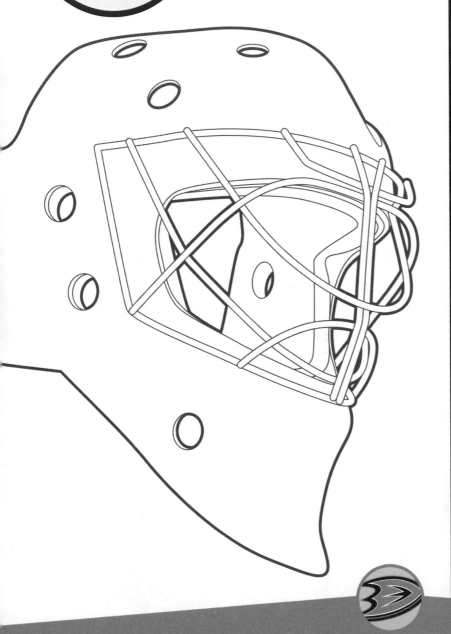

QUIZ

HERE ARE NINE QUESTIONS TO SEE HOW MUCH YOU KNOW ABOUT THOSE PLUCKY DUCKS. GET SIX OR MORE RIGHT AND YOU'RE A STARTER. GET THREE OR LESS AND IT'S BACK TO THE MINORS!

1 In their first decade or so, the Anaheim Ducks were known as the what?

2 Who was the team's first owner?

3 A spectacular 1980-81 season earned Ducks coach Randy Carlyle, then a player with Pittsburgh, what trophy?

4 Ryan Getzlaf's brother Chris plays what sport professionally?

5 In 2011, Corey Perry became just the second Duck to win the Rocket Richard Trophy. Who was the first (hint: his No. 8 has been retired)?

6 When Patrick Eaves was traded to the Ducks, they became his seventh NHL team. Do you remember his first?

7 Which Duck is the NHL's active Iron Man with the most consecutive games played?

8 John Gibson and former Duck Frederick Andersen shared what trophy in 2016?

9 Ducks GM Bob Murray had a long playing career, topping 1,000 games with which team?

WORD SEARCH

```
P  A  N  I  K  N  N  O  S  B  I  G  N
C  A  M  F  O  W  L  E  R  R  M  R  I
Q  R  G  R  E  L  S  E  K  D  S  E  J
F  C  K  G  S  L  L  A  O  S  R  B  K
L  C  O  R  E  Y  P  E  R  R  Y  R  G
Z  L  O  G  L  T  D  H  N  H  A  E  O
K  N  R  R  L  E  Z  O  H  V  R  V  X
E  R  A  K  T  I  S  L  L  A  R  F  A
G  C  A  O  T  N  A  L  A  B  U  L  T
Y  V  A  T  A  N  E  N  E  F  M  I  A
B  W  S  M  K  K  F  F  O  Y  N  S  R
H  O  N  D  A  C  E  N  T  E  R  T  C
C  U  J  R  L  I  N  D  H  O  L  M  E
```

RAKELL
GETZLAF
CARLYLE
MURRAY
KESLER
COREY PERRY
MANSON
LINDHOLM
GIBSON
HONDA CENTER
CAM FOWLER
VATANEN
SILFVERBERG
COGLIANO

JOHN GIBSON #36

FILL IN THE BLANKS

Hidden here is the last name of a current Duck star. Find out who he is by filling in the blank spaces to get the homes of five NHL teams, either the city or state they play in. We've given you a bunch of letters to get you started. Once you've got them all, the Duck star's name will appear in the boxes.

T _ _ _ ☐ A B _ _ Y

V _ _ N _ _ _ _ _ V ☐ R

A ☐ _ _ Z _ _ _ _ A

C _ _ ☐ O _ _ _ _ _ A

C _ _ _ _ G _ _ R ☐

PUZZLE & QUIZ SOLUTIONS ON PAGE 194

BY THE NUMBERS

Anaheim's Rickard Rakell was at his best with everything on the line last season, as he netted a league-high 10 game-winners. The Ducks won 46 games, meaning Rakell scored the winning goal in nearly 16, 18, 20 or 22 percent of their wins?

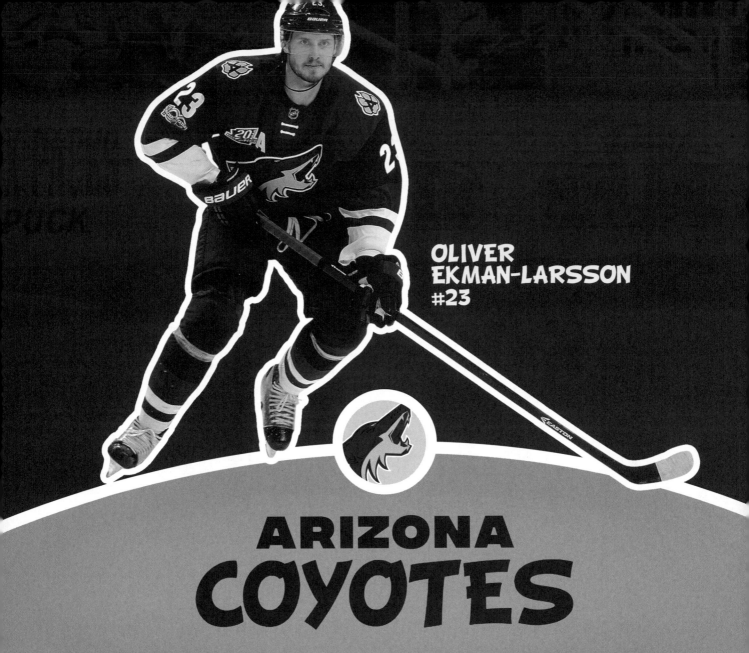

OLIVER EKMAN-LARSSON #23

ARIZONA COYOTES

TIMES HAVE BEEN TOUGH FOR THE COYOTES, who have had more luck finding water in the dry Arizona desert than they have reaching the playoffs. However, the Coyotes have been building for the future by adding young players with all-star potential. The only problem is their plan hasn't worked out so far.

In fact, over the past three seasons, the Coyotes have been so bad that fans have been howling for change. Since the start of the 2013-14 season, no team has won fewer games than Arizona. That's why the Coyotes made a groundbreaking change in the summer, hiring John Chayka to become the team's GM. At 28 years old, Chayka is the youngest NHL GM ever. He's 13 years younger than Shane Doan, who was the oldest player on the team last season!

As much as losing has hurt the Coyotes, the difficult years have given them the chance to form one of the most promising groups of young players of any team. Their brightest young Yote is Max Domi. The son of former Toronto Maple Leafs enforcer Tie Domi, Max has his dad's toughness and in-your-face attitude, but he also has blazing speed and magician-like puck skills. In just two seasons, he's already become a fan favorite in Arizona.

But Domi still has a ways to go before he's the Coyotes' best player. Right now that title belongs to Oliver Ekman-Larsson, a silky smooth defenseman who looks as if he could do his job in his sleep. Even though he plays on the blueline, Ekman-Larsson was the Coyotes' second-highest scorer, with 39 points.

All the young talent couldn't help Arizona get back to the playoffs in 2016-17, but the Coyotes hope their young pups will have them barking up the right tree in the near future.

LEADERS

POINTS
RADIM VRBATA
55

GOALS
RADIM VRBATA
20

ASSISTS
RADIM VRBATA
35

PENALTY MINUTES
LUKE SCHENN
85

ICE TIME
OLIVER EKMAN-LARSSON
24:36

GOALS-AGAINST AVERAGE
MIKE SMITH
2.92

SAVE PERCENTAGE
MIKE SMITH
.914

PRESIDENT ANTHONY LEBLANC
GENERAL MANAGER JOHN CHAYKA
COACH RICK TOCCHET
MASCOT HOWLER THE COYOTE

RECORD
30-42-10

HOME
18-18-5

AWAY
12-24-5

POINTS
70

GOALS FOR
191

GOALS AGAINST
258

AVERAGE AGE
26.0

ROOKIES
5

TOP PROSPECT
CLAYTON KELLER
C, 19,
ACQUIRED:
2016 DRAFT,
7TH OVERALL

HOME JERSEY

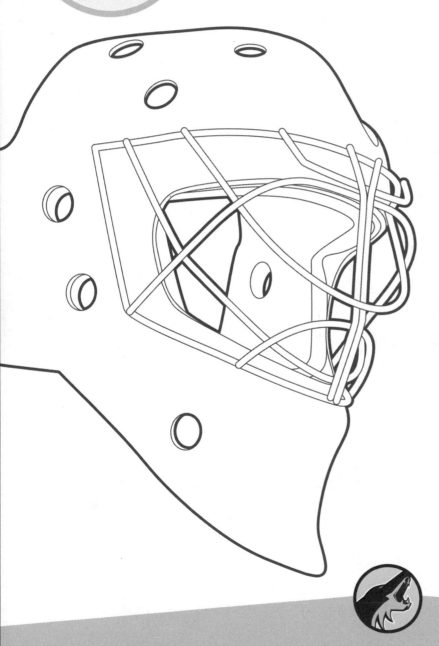

DRAW YOUR OWN MASK

QUIZ

HERE ARE NINE QUESTIONS TO SEE HOW MUCH YOU KNOW ABOUT THE DESERT-DWELLING COYOTES. GET SIX OR MORE RIGHT AND YOU'RE A STARTER. GET THREE OR LESS AND IT'S BACK TO THE MINORS!

1 True or false? Shane Doan was with the franchise when it was based in Winnipeg (the team relocated in 1996).

2 Doan assumed the captaincy back in 2003, 2005 or 2007?

3 What legendary player coached the Coyotes from 2005 to 2009?

4 Former Coyotes coach Dave Tippett previously coached what other Central Division team?

5 How many times has former Coyote Radim Vrbata played for Arizona?

6 Luke Schenn's younger brother, known as 'Little Schenn,' is with St. Louis. What's his name?

7 Mike Smith was the last NHL goalie to do what (hint: Martin Brodeur did it three times)?

8 One Coyote has a luxury clothing line called OEL. Who's that (hint: check out those initials and that should tell you)?

9 Max Domi is the son of what former tough guy?

WORD SEARCH

```
S  D  O  M  I  N  G  U  E  R  T  O  R
N  E  N  N  E  H  C  S  K  K  M  E  E
E  T  E  O  A  V  I  H  M  M  I  T  V
N  I  R  I  E  D  E  R  A  C  S  N  I
U  P  K  L  R  E  A  X  N  Y  E  E  R
R  P  F  S  L  Y  D  T  L  W  K  K  A
H  E  Y  O  O  O  L  A  A  M  R  A  L
C  T  E  M  M  G  E  E  R  B  O  R  I
Y  T  N  I  B  I  I  R  S  S  R  O  G
H  A  T  N  O  I  G  L  S  S  L  V  N
C  N  S  H  A  N  E  D  O  A  N  D  R
R  E  C  D  M  O  D  N  N  G  O  E  B
L  W  I  E  H  T  I  M  S  E  K  I  M
```

SHANE DOAN
TIPPETT
CHAYKA
EKMAN-LARSSON
VRBATA
GILA RIVER
MAX DOMI
DVORAK
SCHENN
MIKE SMITH
DOMINGUE
CHYCHRUN
RIEDER
GOLIGOSKI

LOUIS DOMINGUE #35

FILL IN THE BLANKS

Hidden here is the last name of a current Coyote star. Find out who he is by filling in the blank spaces to get the nicknames of six NHL teams. We've given you a bunch of letters for each team to get you started. Once you've got them all, the Coyote star's name will appear in the boxes from top to bottom.

R _ _ ☐ W _ _ _ _ S

D _ _ ☐ I _ S

S _ N _ _ _ ☐ _ S

S _ B ☐ _ S

F _ ☐ M _ S

D _ _ _ ☐ S

PUZZLE & QUIZ SOLUTIONS ON PAGE 194

BY THE NUMBERS

Jeremy Roenick is one of six Coyotes to have his number retired. If you take all the team's other retired numbers – 7, 9, 10, 25 and 27 – you still have to add 19 more to get J.R.'s number. What is it?

PATRICE
BERGERON
#37

BOSTON BRUINS

FANS IN BOSTON HAD GROWN USED TO watching the big, bad Bruins beat down opponents, but in recent years the winning ways associated with the rough-and-tough team have gone missing. That's why Boston entered the 2016-17 season with one goal in mind: make the playoffs for the first time in three years. It wasn't that Boston hadn't come close in the past – they missed the playoffs by one lousy point in 2015-16 – but this was supposed to be the season that the Bruins climbed the mountain and roared once again.

Things didn't start so smoothly, though. By the midpoint of the season, the Bruins were outside of a playoff spot and desperate to turn their season around. That's when they fired longtime coach Claude Julien, who only days later shocked the hockey world when he was hired by the archrival Montreal Canadiens.

With Julien gone and Bruce Cassidy taking over, the Bruins found a spark. Led by pesky winger Brad Marchand, lovingly referred to as 'The Little Ball of Hate,' the offense caught fire. Marchand was as physical and feisty as ever, and he had the Midas Touch with the puck on his stick. It seemed everything he shot was golden! Meanwhile, 20-year-old winger David Pas-

trnak announced himself as the new kid in town, leaving opposing defenses wide-eyed with his scoring touch.

Boston's old hands were as steady as ever, too. Center Patrice Bergeron, a beast at both ends of the ice, had another top-shelf season, and mountainous 40-year-old defenseman Zdeno Chara turned back the clock. He took on all the important minutes on the Boston blueline, providing goaltender Tuukka Rask with a giant-sized defensive shield.

And when all was said and done, the Bruins managed to bear down and roar back into the playoff hunt, achieving their goal five days before the end of the season.

LEADERS

POINTS
BRAD MARCHAND
85

GOALS
BRAD MARCHAND
39

ASSISTS
BRAD MARCHAND
46

PENALTY MINUTES
BRAD MARCHAND
81

ICE TIME
ZDENO CHARA
23:19

GOALS-AGAINST AVERAGE
TUUKKA RASK
2.23

SAVE PERCENTAGE
TUUKKA RASK
.915

PRESIDENT CAM NEELY
GENERAL MANAGER DON SWEENEY
COACH BRUCE CASSIDY
MASCOT BLADES THE BRUIN

RECORD
44-31-7

HOME
23-17-1

AWAY
21-14-6

POINTS
95

GOALS FOR
232

GOALS AGAINST
209

AVERAGE AGE
28.8

ROOKIES
3

TOP
PROSPECT
CHARLIE MCAVOY
D, 19,
ACQUIRED:
2016 DRAFT,
14TH OVERALL

HOME JERSEY

DRAW YOUR OWN MASK

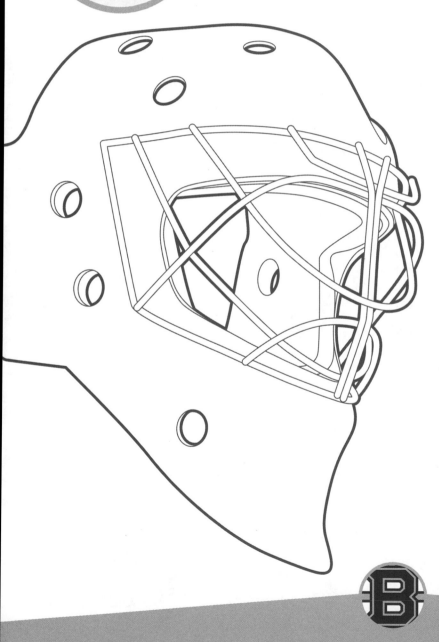

QUIZ

HERE ARE NINE QUESTIONS TO SEE HOW MUCH YOU KNOW ABOUT THE BOSTON BRUINS. GET SIX OR MORE RIGHT AND YOU'RE A STARTER. GET THREE OR LESS AND IT'S BACK TO THE MINORS!

1 Zdeno Chara is the tallest player ever in the NHL. How tall is he?

2 Two other teams gave up on Chara before he came to Boston. Which two?

3 Which Bruin did former president Barack Obama refer to as a 'Little Ball of Hate' when the team visited the White House after winning the Stanley Cup?

4 Goalie Tuukka Rask rarely sits out a game. The past three seasons, he's played an average of how many games (hint: it's 'Super Mario's' old number)?

5 You know that old guy who dresses funny on Coach's Corner – he once coached the Bruins. What's his name?

6 Boston's arena has been known by a handful of names. What's it called now (hint: it's named after a Canadian bank)?

7 Harvard-schooled Dominic Moore was with the Bruins last season after stints with how many other NHL teams?

8 One of P.K. Subban's younger brothers, drafted in the first round in 2012, saw a little action with Boston in 2016-17. What's his name?

9 Defenseman Adam McQuaid hails from Canada's tiniest province. What is it?

WORD SEARCH

```
S T K N E D R A G D T S Z
W N E S H R A K A T U J A
E K E F A M A D V I U X R
E N R L L N O N A N K E A
N C L E R T E A T U K K H
E A S T J W G H R K A E C
Y Y S Y D C R C A S R K S
N A P K D D I R N O A U S
P I O L B I A A O S S E G
E U O C I A S M R T K P W
L B N A H M K S H C I E U
G I E E K U B O A E H U J
N O R E G R E B D C D L N
```

CHARA
KREJCI
SWEENEY
MARCHAND
CASSIDY
TD GARDEN
TUUKKA RASK
PASTRNAK
KRUG
MOORE
BACKES
BERGERON
SPOONER
VATRANO

TUUKKA RASK #40

FILL IN THE BLANKS

Hidden here is the last name of a current Bruin star. Find out who he is by filling in the blank spaces to get the homes of five NHL teams, either the city or state they play in. We've given you the first and last letters of each city or state and one or two more to get you started. Once you've got them all, the Bruin star's name will appear in the boxes reading from top to bottom.

C _ _ _ _ ☐ A _ O

W _ _ _ _ ☐ _ _ N G _ _ ON

D ☐ _ _ L _ S

M _ _ N _ _ ☐ _ _ _ _ L

N ☐ S H _ _ _ _ _ _ E

PUZZLE & QUIZ SOLUTIONS ON PAGE 194

BY THE NUMBERS

Boston's Patrice Bergeron was the best faceoff man in the league last season, winning 1,089 of the 1,812 draws he took. That's almost exactly 55 percent, 60 percent or 65 percent?

RYAN
O'REILLY
#90

BUFFALO SABRES

JACK EICHEL WAS A MAN ON A MISSION LAST season. But sadly for Eichel and the Buffalo Sabres, it turned out to be mission impossible.

As the season began, Eichel's assignment was to lead Buffalo to the playoffs for the first time in five seasons and become the scoring star the Sabres hoped he would be when they drafted him second overall in 2015. However, disaster struck just as Eichel's work was about to begin. The morning before the Sabres' first game of the season, he suffered an ankle injury that forced him to miss the first 21 games.

With Eichel gone, Buffalo struggled, and it didn't help that the rest of the Sabres were wounded. The team flocked to the injured list, and there was only one player, veteran captain Brian Gionta, who dressed in all 82 games. That meant some of Buffalo's best players were forced out of action, including Ryan O'Reilly, Sam Reinhart and Kyle Okposo, who was supposed to be Eichel's sharp-shooting winger.

When Eichel eventually made his come-back, he made up for lost time, showing why he's considered the Sabres' franchise player and one of hockey's slickest centers. Eichel stampeded up the scoring charts, setting a career high in points with 57 in just 61 games. When the season ended, Eichel was one of the league's most reliable scorers, av-eraging nearly one point per game. But even though he was sniping his Sabres back up the league's standings, he couldn't saddle up and steer a hot-and-cold Buffalo team into the playoffs.

After missing the post-season for the sixth-straight year, Buffalo fired coach Dan Bylsma and GM Tim Murray. But that doesn't mean the goal has changed for the Sabres. The playoffs are the plan and come next season Eichel's going to do his best to make sure his mission is complete.

LEADERS

POINTS
JACK EICHEL
57 →

GOALS
EVANDER KANE
28

ASSISTS
RASMUS RISTOLAINEN
39

PENALTY MINUTES
EVANDER KANE
113

ICE TIME
RASMUS RISTOLAINEN
26:28

GOALS-AGAINST AVERAGE
ANDERS NILSSON
2.67

SAVE PERCENTAGE
ANDERS NILSSON
.923

PRESIDENT RUSS BRANDON
GENERAL MANAGER JASON BOTTERILL
COACH PHIL HOUSLEY
MASCOT SABRETOOTH

RECORD
33-37-12

HOME
20-15-6

AWAY
13-22-6

POINTS
78

GOALS FOR
199

GOALS AGAINST
231

AVERAGE AGE
26.4

ROOKIES
3

TOP PROSPECT
ALEXANDER NYLANDER
RW, 19,
ACQUIRED:
2016 DRAFT,
8TH OVERALL

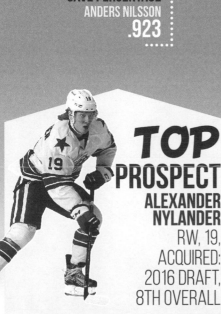

HOME JERSEY

DRAW YOUR OWN MASK

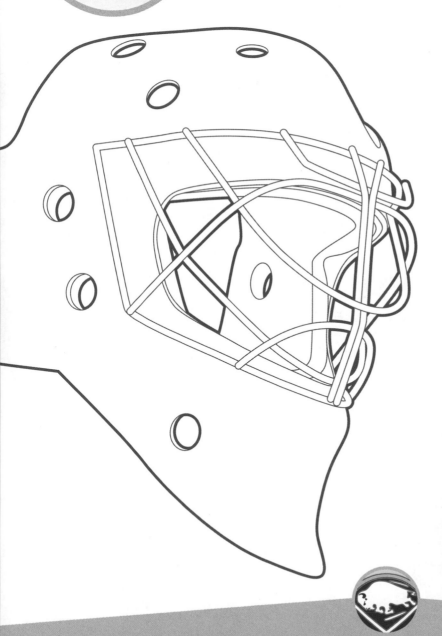

QUIZ

HERE ARE NINE QUESTIONS TO SEE HOW MUCH YOU KNOW ABOUT THE SABRES. GET SIX OR MORE RIGHT AND YOU'RE A STARTER. GET THREE OR LESS AND IT'S BACK TO THE MINORS!

1 Former Buffalo coach Dan Bylsma steered what team to a Stanley Cup in 2009?

2 Bylsma played with two West Coast teams. Which two?

3 He's known as both 'Gio' and the 'Rochester Rocket.' He's also captain in Buffalo. Who is he?

4 Both O'Reilly boys played with the Sabres last season. What are their first names?

5 Which Buffalo goalie is a heavy metal fan?

6 The Sabres arena has had several names. What is it known as now?

7 Which Latvian-born Sabre, with a unique first name, scored in his Olympic debut in 2014?

8 Evander Kane was well regarded entering the 2009 draft and was selected fourth overall by what now-defunct team?

9 Who delivered a crushing hit on Jets rookie Patrik Laine last season, injuring Laine for a couple weeks?

WORD SEARCH

```
S  D  T  R  A  H  N  I  E  R  T  R  E
N  E  L  N  T  I  L  D  E  K  M  E  B
E  V  E  O  A  V  I  N  L  U  I  T  A
N  A  Y  S  S  D  H  J  O  C  S  N  C
I  N  R  L  R  E  K  B  H  J  E  E  C
A  D  F  U  L  Y  C  E  N  W  G  C  M
L  E  Y  O  N  I  L  A  A  M  R  K  I
O  R  E  M  L  N  E  E  M  H  O  N  V
T  K  N  T  B  I  O  R  S  S  G  A  Q
S  A  T  N  O  I  G  H  O  S  L  B  N
I  N  O  G  I  L  B  N  I  A  E  Y  R
R  E  C  D  M  U  D  N  O  M  O  E  B
S  T  H  E  D  O  K  P  O  S  O  K  H
```

EVANDER KANE
GORGES
GIONTA
BYLSMA
KEYBANK CENTER
O'REILLY
OKPOSO
RISTOLAINEN
EICHEL
MCCABE
LEHNER
FOLIGNO
REINHART
MOULSON

ROBIN LEHNER #40

PUZZLE & QUIZ SOLUTIONS ON PAGE 194

FILL IN THE BLANKS

Hidden here is the last name of a current Sabre star. Find out who he is by filling in the blank spaces to get the homes of six NHL teams, either the city or state they play in. We've given you the first and last letters of each city or state and one or two more to get you started. Once you've got them all, the Sabre star's name will appear in the boxes.

C _ _ _ C _ _ ☐ O

W _ _ _ _ _ ☐ P _ _ G

B ☐ _ _ T _ N

T _ _ R _ ☐ _ _ O

O _ _ ☐ A _ _ A

L ☐ _ _ V _ _ _ _ _ S

BY THE NUMBERS

The Buffalo Sabres aren't generally thought of as a rough-and-tumble team, but they did amass a record 2,713 penalty minutes in the 1991-92 season, when teams played 80 games. In contrast, the Flames led the league with just 956 minutes in 2016-17. That's a difference of how many minutes?

SEAN MONAHAN #23

CALGARY FLAMES

A DOWN SEASON IN CALGARY LEFT THE FLAMES with a burning desire to get back to the playoffs in 2016-17, and two star scorers and one feisty young talent made all the difference.

As they have the past few seasons, the Flames were led on offense by Johnny Gaudreau and Sean Monahan, who have gone together like peanut butter and jelly since joining forces in 2014-15. Gaudreau, a left winger, is the speedster of the two, blazing up the ice and beating defensemen with highlight-reel plays almost every single game. Short in height but big in heart, Gaudreau has the most points of any Cal-

gary player since he joined the team. But Monahan, a goal-scoring center, has been right there alongside him. It came as no surprise that Gaudreau and Monahan were first and second in Flames' scoring, but their company atop the scoring charts did turn some heads.

It took rookie Matthew Tkachuk only a few short months after he was drafted to become an impact player for the Flames. Tkachuk, the son of ex-NHLer Keith Tkachuk, was as good as any other Flame last season and became an instant hit among fans in Calgary. Opposing fans didn't love him quite as much, though. His mosquito-like ability

to annoy the opposition made him hard to handle, but he had bite to go with his buzz. When the season ended, Tkachuk was the team's fifth-highest scorer.

But the offensive trio of Gaudreau, Monahan and Tkachuk would have been nothing without a rock-solid defense. Veteran captain Mark Giordano was cool, calm and collected as the team's on-ice leader and young defenseman Dougie Hamilton had the best season of his career, blasting his way to new scoring heights. With new coach Glen Gulutzan pushing all the right buttons, the Flames turned things around in a hurry, reigniting the 'C' of Red.

LEADERS

GOALS
SEAN MONAHAN
27

ASSISTS
JOHNNY GAUDREAU
43

PENALTY MINUTES
MATTHEW TKACHUK
105

ICE TIME
MARK GIORDANO
23:35

GOALS-AGAINST AVERAGE
BRIAN ELLIOTT
2.55

SAVE PERCENTAGE
CHAD JOHNSTON & BRIAN ELLIOTT
.910

POINTS
JOHNNY GAUDREAU
61

PRESIDENT KEN KING
GENERAL MANAGER BRAD TRELIVING
COACH GLEN GULUTZAN
MASCOT HARVEY THE HOUND

RECORD
45-33-4

HOME
24-17-0

AWAY
21-16-4

POINTS
94

GOALS FOR
222

GOALS AGAINST
219

AVERAGE AGE
28.3

ROOKIES
2

TOP
PROSPECT
TYLER PARSONS
G, 20,
ACQUIRED:
2016 DRAFT,
54TH OVERALL

HOME JERSEY

DRAW YOUR OWN MASK

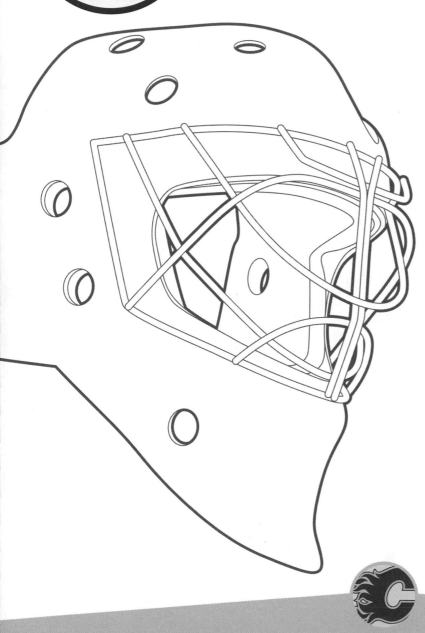

QUIZ

HERE ARE NINE QUESTIONS TO SEE HOW MUCH YOU KNOW ABOUT THE RESURGENT FLAMES. GET SIX OR MORE RIGHT AND YOU'RE A STARTER. GET THREE OR LESS AND IT'S BACK TO THE MINORS!

1 Coach Glen Gulutzan spent a handful of seasons coaching in what gambling mecca (hint: it has now got an NHL team)?

2 Captain Mark Giordano spent a season with what KHL team based in Moscow?

3 The Saddledome is now sponsored by what bank?

4 Goalie Brian Elliott has been around. Can you name at least two of his three former teams?

5 Matthew Tkachuk's dad played more than 1,200 NHL Games. What's his name?

6 Johnny Gaudreau is better known by what nickname?

7 Sean Monahan also starred in what sport as a youngster (hint: it was once Canada's national game)?

8 Kris Versteeg won Stanley Cups with what team in 2010 and again in 2015?

9 Mikael Backlund is a spokesman for what event for the intellectually disabled?

WORD SEARCH

```
E  E  G  A  U  D  R  E  A  U  T  A  Z
L  M  N  A  J  A  T  S  R  D  R  J  E
L  O  G  N  A  R  C  E  N  A  K  X  T
I  D  A  L  L  O  W  A  O  I  P  T  Z
O  E  E  M  R  U  L  A  L  Y  K  R  O
T  L  A  A  O  R  M  O  N  A  H  A  N
T  D  H  R  E  A  R  H  C  U  A  K  A
A  D  B  F  O  F  A  H  H  I  M  R  D
N  A  Z  T  U  L  U  G  C  S  I  L  R
E  S  B  A  C  K  L  U  N  D  L  P  O
F  B  O  A  J  L  K  E  A  A  T  C  I
Y  E  K  C  O  H  Y  N  N  H  O  J  G
C  K  U  A  N  I  F  E  D  O  N  L  R
```

GAUDREAU
JOHNNY HOCKEY
HAMILTON
GULUTZAN
BACKLUND
FERLAND
MONAHAN
TKACHUK
GIORDANO
STAJAN
SADDLEDOME
ELLIOTT
FROLIK
BROUWER

MATTHEW TKACHUK #19

FILL IN THE BLANKS

Hidden here is the last name of a current Flame star. Find out who he is by filling in the blank spaces to get the nicknames of eight NHL teams. We've given you the first and last letters of each team and one or two more to get you started. Once you've got them all, the Flame's name will appear in the boxes reading from top to bottom.

G __ L __ __ __ N K __ __ __ ☐ __ T S

C ☐ __ __ __ C __ S

B __ __ ☐ __ S

I __ __ __ A __ __ ☐ __ __ __ S

O __ __ L __ __ ☐ S

S __ __ B __ __ ☐ S

P ☐ N __ H __ __ __ S

D ☐ __ __ __ S

PUZZLE & QUIZ SOLUTIONS ON PAGE 194

BY THE NUMBERS

The once mild-mannered Flames got angry in 2016-17, as they led the NHL in penalty minutes, piling up 956 minutes in 82 games? Roughly how many penalty minutes per game is that?

JORDAN STAAL #11

CAROLINA HURRICANES

ENTERING THE 2016-17 SEASON WITH THE fourth-youngest roster and a few exciting new faces gave the Hurricanes hope, but for the second-straight season, Swiss cheese goaltending hung over Carolina like a storm cloud.

With Eddie Lack and Cam Ward in goal, it appeared the nets were soccer-sized for opposing shooters, and on some nights it seemed neither netminder could have stopped a beach ball. On the best nights, Carolina got average goaltending, but the bad nights were downright awful. Even coach Bill Peters was begging for someone, anyone to make a save.

But the Hurricanes still nearly shocked the league, making a playoff push late in the season. For that reason alone, the future looks bright in Carolina.

As always, it was Jeff Skinner, the small, slippery sniper, who was the team's best scorer. Skinner used his figure skating background to dipsy-doodle on the ice, dancing around defenders and slipping pucks past even the best stoppers on his way to finishing with the sixth-most goals in the league.

What surprised Hurricanes fans, however, was rookie Sebastian Aho. The 19-year-old didn't earn as many headlines as a few of his fellow first-year players, but the swift-skat-

ing, whip-smart winger showed he had the talent to compete with even the biggest, brightest stars in the NHL. In just his first year, he finished second on the team in scoring and was the fifth-highest scoring rookie in the league.

GM Ron Francis, who is also the Hurricanes' all-time leading scorer, has set Carolina up for future success, too, adding support players like center Victor Rask, winger Teuvo Teravainen and blueliners such as Jaccob Slavin, Noah Hanifin and Brett Pesce. Even with the subpar goaltending, the winds of change seem to be blowing in the right direction for the Hurricanes.

LEADERS

POINTS
JEFF SKINNER
63

GOALS
JEFF SKINNER
37

ASSISTS
ELIAS LINDHOLM
34

PENALTY MINUTES
JORDAN STAAL
38

ICE TIME
JACCOB SLAVIN
23:26

GOALS-AGAINST AVERAGE
EDDIE LACK
2.64

SAVE PERCENTAGE
CAM WARD
.905

PRESIDENT DON WADDELL
GENERAL MANAGER RON FRANCIS
COACH BILL PETERS
MASCOT STORMY

RECORD
36-31-15

HOME
23-12-6

AWAY
13-19-9

POINTS
87

GOALS FOR
212

GOALS AGAINST
230

AVERAGE AGE
26.8

ROOKIES
2

TOP
PROSPECT
JULIEN GAUTHIER
RW, 20,
ACQUIRED:
2016 DRAFT,
21ST OVERALL

HOME JERSEY

DRAW YOUR OWN MASK

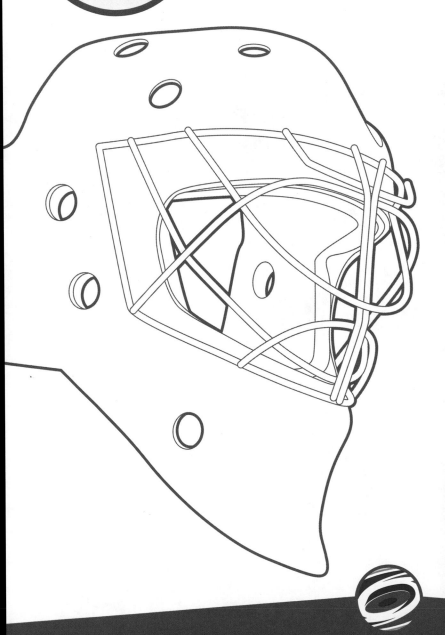

QUIZ

HERE ARE NINE QUESTIONS TO SEE HOW MUCH YOU KNOW ABOUT THE HURRICANES. GET SIX OR MORE RIGHT AND YOU'RE A STARTER. GET THREE OR LESS AND IT'S BACK TO THE MINORS!

1 Coach Bill Peters was previously an assistant with which NHL team?

2 Goalie Cam Ward was in his first, second or third NHL season when he hoisted the Stanley Cup with Carolina in 2006?

3 Which Cane is the youngest to play in the NHL All-Star Game?

4 This player went on to win what trophy in 2011?

5 The Hurricanes have a lot of players with short last names, but this player's is the shortest at just three letters. Who is he?

6 Jordan Staal was nicknamed 'Gronk' after a comic book supervillain while playing for what team?

7 Who did Ron Francis succeed as GM in 2014?

8 Teuvo Teravainen's dad has an interesting occupation, especially considering his son is a hockey player. What does he do (hint: he can fix your "chiclets")?

9 What were the Hurricanes called when the team was based in Hartford?

WORD SEARCH

```
E  S  C  W  B  B  F  L  E  M  A  S  U
S  I  A  N  E  R  A  C  N  P  T  R  I
J  C  M  S  E  E  T  R  Y  A  E  E  V
K  N  W  T  L  T  K  X  A  H  N  T  R
R  A  A  E  E  T  I  L  H  S  R  E  T
T  R  R  M  S  P  D  B  U  A  K  P  Y
I  F  D  P  U  E  E  N  C  A  C  L  N
O  N  U  N  I  S  N  E  H  E  F  L  O
S  O  R  I  L  C  K  O  S  P  U  I  S
A  R  I  A  R  E  N  N  I  K  S  B  C
M  P  V  K  U  L  I  N  D  H  O  L  M
C  I  R  M  S  X  A  E  R  I  N  S  I
N  E  N  E  N  I  A  V  A  R  E  T  E
```

BILL PETERS
FAULK
RASK
SKINNER
STAAL
PNC ARENA
LINDHOLM
CAM WARD
AHO
TERAVAINEN
RON FRANCIS
BRETT PESCE
SLAVIN
STEMPNIAK

CAM
WARD
#30

FILL IN THE BLANKS

Hidden here is the last name of a current Hurricane star. Find out who he is by filling in the blank spaces to get the homes of five NHL teams, either the city or state they play in. We've given you the first and last letters of each city or state and one or two more to get you started. Once you've got them all, the Hurricane star's name will appear in the boxes reading from top to bottom.

B __ □ T __ N

O __ □ A __ A

N □ S H __ __ __ __ __ __ E

C __ __ C □ __ O

C __ □ G __ __ __ Y

PUZZLE & QUIZ SOLUTIONS ON PAGE 194

BY THE NUMBERS

Unlike the feisty Anaheim Ducks, who had 46 fighting majors last season, the Hurricanes were the least likely to mix it up in 2016-17, with just 6 scraps. On average, how many games is that per fight?

JONATHAN
TOEWS
#19

CHICAGO
BLACKHAWKS

CONTINUING ON AS THE CONFERENCE'S powerhouse is never easy, but the Chicago Blackhawks had the help of their star-studded core to guide them through the 2016-17 season. And leave it to Patrick Kane, the league's defending MVP, to be the team's leading scorer again. Kane is so talented he seems to undress the best defensemen in the league with ease, spinning them into the ice with dekes so eye-popping fans can be faked out of their seats. Last season saw Kane continue to have an almost psychic connection with Artemi Panarin. Kane put pucks on a platter for Panarin, who blasted one-timers with pinpoint accuracy.

It wasn't enough to keep Panarin in Chicago, though. He was traded to Columbus in the off-season for Brandon Saad, who returns for his second stint as a Hawk. Rookies Ryan Hartman and Nick Schmaltz weren't at the top of the Blackhawks' scoring charts, but both showed signs of becoming the type of players who can help Chicago stay on top. Hartman made his mark as a consistent scorer and agitating force, while Schmaltz, considered a future star for the Blackhawks, came to life in the second half of the season. Paired with captain Jonathan Toews, Schmaltz made some magic, and pucks started to appear in the back of opposing teams nets.

But the backbone for the Windy City's on-ice warriors was goaltender Corey Crawford. Often underrated, Crawford had another outstanding season in the Blackhawks' crease, turning in stonewall performances on a near nightly basis. Some games even a cannon blast wouldn't have gotten by Chicago's caged crusader!

Unfortunately for fans, their beloved Hawks lost in the first round of the playoffs to the Nashville Predators. The Blackhawks continue to look to add to their modern-day dynasty, though, and this all-star cast with some skillful new skaters won't rest until they add a seventh Stanley Cup to Chicago's trophy case.

LEADERS

POINTS
PATRICK KANE
89

GOALS
PATRICK KANE
34

ASSISTS
PATRICK KANE
55

PENALTY MINUTES
RYAN HARTMAN
70

ICE TIME
DUNCAN KEITH
25:37

GOALS-AGAINST AVERAGE
SCOTT DARLING
2.38

SAVE PERCENTAGE
SCOTT DARLING
.924

PRESIDENT JOHN F. MCDONOUGH
GENERAL MANAGER STAN BOWMAN
COACH JOEL QUENNEVILLE
MASCOT TOMMY HAWK

RECORD
50-23-9

HOME
26-10-5

AWAY
24-13-4

POINTS
109

GOALS FOR
240

GOALS AGAINST
212

AVERAGE AGE
29.4

ROOKIES
6

TOP
PROSPECT
ALEX DEBRINCAT
RW, 19,
ACQUIRED:
2016 DRAFT,
39TH OVERALL

HOME JERSEY

CHICAGO BLACKHAWKS **77**

DRAW YOUR OWN MASK

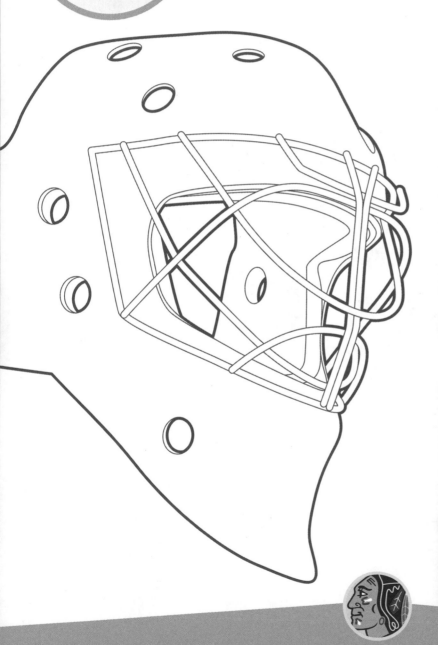

QUIZ

HERE ARE NINE QUESTIONS TO SEE HOW MUCH YOU KNOW ABOUT THE BLACKHAWKS. GET SIX OR MORE RIGHT AND YOU'RE A STARTER. GET THREE OR LESS AND IT'S BACK TO THE MINORS!

1 Joel Quenneville has been the coach in Chicago for a while. What legendary Blackhawk did he take over for?

2 How many Stanley Cups did Bobby Hull and Stan Mikita win while with Chicago?

3 Who did the Blackhawks pick first overall in 2007?

4 Who was Chicago's first Conn Smythe Trophy winner?

5 Who was the team's most recent Smythe winner?

6 Which Hawk is nicknamed 'Crow'?

7 Before finally winning a Cup with Chicago in 2010, Marian Hossa lost in the final the previous two seasons with different clubs. Can you name the two teams?

8 One Blackhawk's last name is defined in the dictionary as meaning "excessive sentimentality." Who is it?

9 John Hayden is a hometown boy. So, where was he born?

WORD SEARCH

```
P  A  N  I  K  N  I  R  A  N  A  P  N
L  C  E  O  L  E  J  A  S  R  M  A  I
J  R  G  N  I  L  R  A  D  D  S  T  B
F  A  K  C  S  L  G  A  O  S  R  R  K
L  W  O  R  K  I  I  A  O  C  V  I  U
O  F  O  A  O  V  D  H  N  H  O  C  H
S  O  R  D  P  E  O  H  H  M  M  K  E
A  R  B  K  T  N  N  T  I  A  I  K  R
R  D  A  O  T  N  I  R  S  L  S  A  T
Z  R  E  T  N  E  C  D  E  T  I  N  U
E  W  S  D  K  U  F  F  I  Z  N  E  R
S  E  T  N  E  Q  S  E  L  P  A  T  S
C  H  J  A  L  M  A  R  S  S  O  N  E
```

HOSSA
QUENNEVILLE
TOEWS
KEITH
SEABROOK
UNITED CENTER
PATRICK KANE
CRAWFORD
DARLING
PANARIN
PANIK
HJALMARSSON
SCHMALTZ
ANISIMOV

COREY CRAWFORD #50

FILL IN THE BLANKS

Hidden here is the last name of a current Blackhawk star. Find out who he is by filling in the blank spaces to get the homes of five NHL teams, either the city or state they play in. We've given you a bunch of letters to get you started. Once you've got them all, the Blackhawk star's name will appear in the boxes reading from top to bottom.

N __ W Y __ R ☐

P ___ L __ D ☐ _____ A

P ☐ ___ S _____ H

B __ S ☐ __ N

N __ S ☐ ___ L __ E

PUZZLE & QUIZ SOLUTIONS ON PAGE 195

BY THE NUMBERS

The Blackhawks have retired a few numbers, including 1, 3, 9, 18 and 21. If you add those up, you get the record number of wins posted by Chicago in a season (in 2009-10). How many was it?

MATT
DUCHENE
#9

COLORADO
AVALANCHE

IF A BOOK WERE WRITTEN ABOUT COLORADO'S 2016-17 season, it would be called *The Colorado Avalanche and the Terrible, Horrible, No Good, Very Bad Season*. Anything that could have gone wrong in Denver did, and the Avalanche couldn't have been happier to see the season end.

The signs were there from the start, too. Before the season began, Colorado had to scramble to find a new coach after Patrick Roy, the Hall of Famer turned Avalanche coach, decided to quit. Only weeks later, Colorado announced the hiring of Jared Bednar, who had won the American Hockey League championship just two months earlier. Sadly Bednar's memories of his rookie coaching campaign are going to be pretty rotten.

Things didn't start out too badly for the Avalanche as they won their first two games, but the success didn't last long and Colorado began to roll down the standings. First came one loss, followed by another and then things snowballed out of control.

The Avalanche went through several long losing streaks, the longest being nine games! When the season came to a close, Colorado finished with the worst record in the league, winning only 22 games and earning 48 points. It was the fewest points a team had earned over a full season in the past 15 years.

If there was one glimmer of hope for the Avalanche, it came from the play of rookie Mikko Rantanen and late-season addition Tyson Jost. Rantanen was Colorado's only player to score 20 goals. As for Jost, he joined the Avalanche with six games left in the season, scoring his first career goal in just his fourth game.

Changes are coming in Colorado, but the failures of last season will become a distant memory if the likes of Rantanen and Jost can lead the Avalanche forward.

LEADERS

POINTS
NATHAN MACKINNON
53

GOALS
MIKKO RANTANEN
20

ASSISTS
NATHAN MACKINNON
37

PENALTY MINUTES
NIKITA ZADOROV
73

ICE TIME
TYSON BARRIE
23:18

GOALS-AGAINST AVERAGE
CALVIN PICKARD
2.98

SAVE PERCENTAGE
CALVIN PICKARD
.904

PRESIDENT JOSH KROENKE
GENERAL MANAGER JOE SAKIC
COACH JARED BEDNAR
MASCOT BERNIE THE ST. BERNARD

RECORD
22-56-4

HOME
13-26-2

AWAY
9-30-2

POINTS
48

GOALS FOR
165

GOALS AGAINST
276

AVERAGE AGE
27.6

ROOKIES
1

TOP
PROSPECT
TYSON JOST
C, 19,
ACQUIRED:
2016 DRAFT,
10TH OVERALL

HOME JERSEY

DRAW YOUR OWN MASK

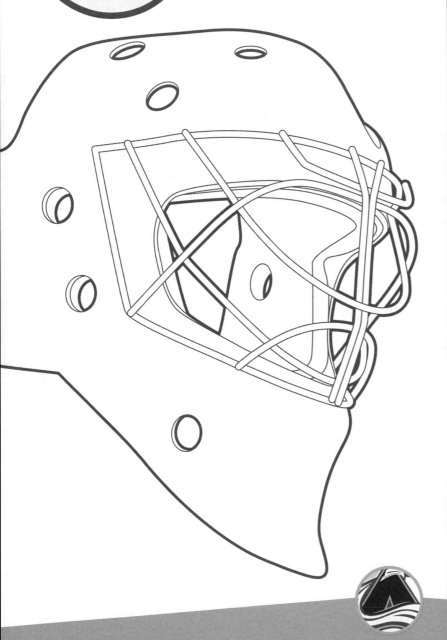

QUIZ

HERE ARE NINE QUESTIONS TO SEE HOW MUCH YOU KNOW ABOUT THE AVALANCHE. GET SIX OR MORE RIGHT AND YOU'RE A STARTER. GET THREE OR LESS AND IT'S BACK TO THE MINORS!

1 Where did the Avalanche initially call home (hint: it's in Canada)?

2 GM Joe Sakic had quite the playing career. How many Cups did he win with Colorado?

3 Sakic is in both the Hockey Hall of Fame and in what Calgary-based Hall?

4 Gabriel Landeskog was named Avalanche captain at the ripe young age of 19, 20, 21 or 22?

5 What soft drink company sponsors Colorado's arena?

6 Two weeks after Patrick Roy resigned as coach, who did the Avs hire to take his place?

7 Colorado drafted Nathan MacKinnon first, second or third overall in 2013?

8 Former Avs goalie Calvin Pickard represented Canada at the 2016 World Championship in Russia. What medal did he take home?

9 Carl Soderberg played in the Swedish Hockey League with his hometown team, the Redhawks. What city are they based in?

WORD SEARCH

```
L M N I M E H C U A E B N
L A E O L E N E H C U D I
J Z N T H E C H I N F C C
S Z A D M A C K I N N O N
O I T D E U A A R S W L S
D N N A O S P I C K A R D
E E A D E R K H J A H A O
R S R O I R O O I E U N R
B I J O T S H V G P P D R
E U R E T N E C I S P E P
R B E D S O F F I L C B R
G E B O U R Q U E P A T S
C A N D R I G H E T T O F
```

LANDESKOG
DUCHENE
BEDNAR
PEPSI CENTER
RANTANEN
MACKINNON
JOE SAKIC
ZADOROV
PICKARD
ANDRIGHETTO
BOURQUE
SODERBERG
JOHNSON
BEAUCHEMIN

SEMYON VARLAMOV #1

FILL IN THE BLANKS

Hidden here is the last name of a current Avalanche star. Find out who he is by filling in the blank spaces to get the homes of nine NHL teams, either the city or state they play in. We've given you a bunch of letters to get you started. Once you've got them all, the Avalanche star's name will appear in the boxes reading from top to bottom.

```
P __ I □ A __ __ __ __ __ __ H __ A
A __ □ H __ __ M
W __ N □ __ __ __ __ G
E □ __ __ __ __ T __ N
M __ __ __ T __ □ __ L
L __ □ V __ __ __ __ S
N __ W YO __ □
S __ N J □ __ E
W __ __ H __ __ □ T __ N
```

PUZZLE & QUIZ SOLUTIONS ON PAGE 195

BY THE NUMBERS

Joe Sakic is now GM in Colorado, but he had a long career with the Avalanche and was captain from 1992 to 2008. How many years is that?

NICK FOLIGNO #71

COLUMBUS BLUE JACKETS

AFTER THE WAY HE PERFORMED IN 2016-17, Sergei Bobrovsky may have convinced fans in Columbus that his surname is Russian for "brick wall."

Recent seasons hadn't been kind to Bobrovsky, but the Blue Jackets netminder was at the top of his game in 2016-17. There's almost no question Bobrovsky was the best goaltender in the league, practically sleepwalking his way through the easy saves and making the toughest stops look like a walk in the park. With lightning-fast reflexes and a can't-be-beat mentality, Bobrovsky shut the door on a nightly basis and led the league in nearly every major goaltending catego-

ry. And his play made a massive difference in Columbus.

Backstopped by Bobrovsky and led by fiery coach John Tortorella, the Blue Jackets posted the best record in franchise history, winning 50 games and earning a whopping 108 points. A big part of Columbus' outstanding record was a mindboggling winning streak. Beginning with a victory against the Tampa Bay Lightning on Nov. 29, the Blue Jackets went on a 16-game winning streak, even ending a 12-game winning streak by the Minnesota Wild along the way. The Jackets' streak wasn't snapped until Jan. 3, as they came one victory shy of tying the

1992-93 Pittsburgh Penguins' NHL record of 17 wins in a row.

Offensively, Columbus' winning ways were powered by scoring surge of Cam Atkinson, who fired home an outstanding 35 goals, as well as 20-goal scorers Nick Foligno and Brandon Saad, who was traded to Chicago for Artemi Panarin in the off-season. Meanwhile, rookie Zach Werenski turned heads on the blueline with his rock-solid play, becoming a Calder Trophy finalist as one of the league's top rookies. And with the incredible streak rocketing the club up the standings, the Blue Jackets were in the perfect position to earn their first trip to the playoffs in three seasons.

LEADERS

GOALS
CAM ATKINSON
35

ASSISTS
ALEXANDER WENNBERG
46

PENALTY MINUTES
BRANDON DUBINSKY
91

ICE TIME
SETH JONES
23:24

GOALS-AGAINST AVERAGE
SERGEI BOBROVSKY
2.06

SAVE PERCENTAGE
SERGEI BOBROVSKY
.931

POINTS
CAM ATKINSON
62

PRESIDENT JOHN DAVIDSON
GENERAL MANAGER JARMO KEKALAINEN
COACH JOHN TORTORELLA
MASCOT STINGER

RECORD
50-24-8

HOME
28-12-1

AWAY
22-12-7

POINTS
108

GOALS FOR
247

GOALS AGAINST
193

AVERAGE AGE
26.2

ROOKIES
4

TOP
PROSPECT
PIERRE-LUC DUBOIS
C, 19,
ACQUIRED:
2016 DRAFT,
3RD OVERALL

HOME JERSEY

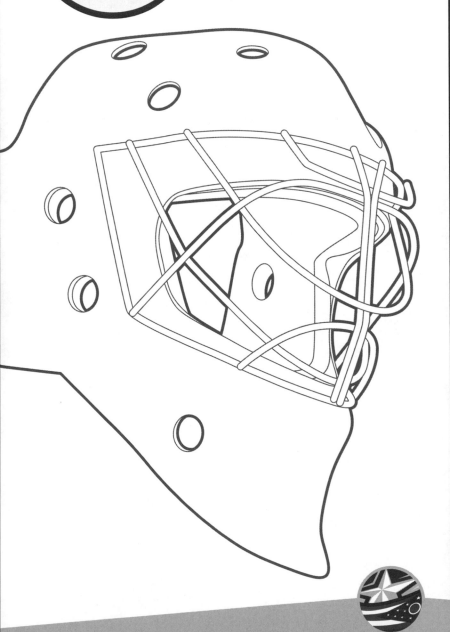

DRAW YOUR OWN MASK

QUIZ

HERE ARE NINE QUESTIONS TO SEE HOW MUCH YOU KNOW ABOUT THE KIDS FROM COLUMBUS. GET SIX OR MORE RIGHT AND YOU'RE A STARTER. GET THREE OR LESS AND IT'S BACK TO THE MINORS!

1 What exactly is a Blue Jacket?

2 John Tortorella has had a stormy coaching career at times, but he did win a Stanley Cup. What team was it with?

3 Captain Nick Foligno is the son of what former Buffalo Sabres captain?

4 What smallish Blue Jacket took over for an injured Evgeni Malkin at the 2017 All-Star Game in Nashville?

5 Former Blue Jacket Brandon Saad still has relatives living in what war-torn country?

6 Which Blue Jacket was honored by Russian president Vladimir Putin?

7 Nationwide Arena is named after what kind of company?

8 Brandon Dubinksy was born in what American city (hint: it's in Alaska)?

9 Former Blue Jacket Sam Gagner was drafted sixth overall by which team in 2007?

WORD SEARCH

```
N  E  G  A  N  I  J  S  A  W  E  N  Z
O  W  E  N  N  B  E  R  G  D  K  J  E
S  O  D  N  A  R  N  L  N  U  K  X  T
N  D  I  N  O  S  N  I  K  T  A  E  V
H  E  W  W  E  R  E  N  S  K  I  H  D
O  F  N  N  O  I  R  O  O  A  E  A  U
J  T  O  R  T  O  R  E  L  L  A  R  B
D  J  I  L  S  F  J  S  T  S  W  T  I
O  R  T  O  I  L  E  G  Y  S  I  N  N
K  S  A  A  E  G  T  E  M  D  L  E  S
T  B  N  V  V  H  N  E  R  K  S  L  K
Y  E  K  N  A  S  E  O  A  H  C  L  Y
M  U  D  Y  K  S  V  O  R  B  O  B  E
```

TORTORELLA
FOLIGNO
DUBINSKY
JENNER
NATIONWIDE
ATKINSON
WENNBERG
SAVARD
BOBROVSKY
WERENSKI
JONES
HARTNELL
JOHNSON
SAAD

SERGEI
BOBROVSKY
#72

FILL IN THE BLANKS

Hidden here is the last name of a current Blue Jacket star. Find out who he is by filling in the blank spaces to get the homes of seven NHL teams, either the city or state they play in. We've given you a bunch of letters to get you started. Once you've got them all, the Blue Jacket star's name will appear in the boxes reading from top to bottom.

B _ _ F ☐ _ _ _ O

M ☐ N _ _ _ _ _ L

D _ _ L ☐ _ S

P ☐ _ _ _ S _ _ _ _ H

C _ _ _ C _ _ ☐ O

C _ R _ _ _ _ ☐ A

C ☐ _ _ M _ _ S

PUZZLE & QUIZ SOLUTIONS ON PAGE 195

BY THE NUMBERS

Sergei Bobrovsky allowed just 127 goals in 63 games last season. Roughly how many goals against is that per game?

JAMIE
BENN
#14

DALLAS STARS

FALLING ONE WIN SHORT OF THE WESTERN Conference final in 2015-16 really hurt, but the Dallas Stars entered the 2016-17 season with hopes higher than scorching Texas temperatures. Unfortunately, injuries, an underperforming defense and terrible goaltending threw cold water on what was supposed to be a successful season.

Before the season began, the injury bug stung the Stars hard. Captain Jamie Benn had to unexpectedly undergo surgery to repair a muscle injury, Ales Hemsky was sidelined with a groin injury and Cody Eakin was put out of action with a bad knee. Dallas' situation got worse, too, when days

before the season was set to begin, a knee injury cost up-and-coming winger Mattias Janmark his entire year. Even mysterious illnesses were attacking the Stars, as off-season signing Jiri Hudler was out for a month with an unknown sickness.

Even when the Stars were healthy, however, it seemed nothing could go right for them. Dan Hamhuis, Dallas' big free agent signing, was expected to be the missing piece on the blueline, but he was benched twice in the first quarter of the season, while the rest of the defense was like a revolving door, letting opposition shooters walk in on goal with ease.

Meanwhile, for the second-straight season, the duo of Kari Lehtonen and Antti Niemi was eaten alive between the pipes. The only team that allowed more goals against was the last-place Colorado Avalanche.

The slick-shooting, run-and-gun Dallas offense was still firing bullets, though. Despite a down season, the Stars still managed to blast home 222 goals, led by a pair of 26-goal seasons from Benn and Tyler Seguin. And while it may have been a disappointing season, the five-star snipers that dot the Dallas lineup give hope that a Texas-sized turnaround is on its way.

LEADERS

POINTS
TYLER SEGUIN
72 ➤➤

GOALS
JAMIE BENN
26

ASSISTS
TYLER SEGUIN
46

PENALTY MINUTES
ANTOINE ROUSSEL
115

ICE TIME
JOHN KLINGBERG
23:21

GOALS-AGAINST AVERAGE
KARI LEHTONEN
2.85

SAVE PERCENTAGE
KARI LEHTONEN
.902

PRESIDENT JIM LITES
GENERAL MANAGER JIM NILL
COACH KEN HITCHCOCK
MASCOT VICTOR E. GREEN

RECORD
34-37-11

HOME
22-13-6

AWAY
12-24-5

POINTS
79

GOALS FOR
222

GOALS AGAINST
260

AVERAGE AGE
27.5

ROOKIES
3

TOP PROSPECT
MIRO HEISKANEN
D, 18,
ACQUIRED:
2017 DRAFT,
3RD OVERALL

HOME JERSEY

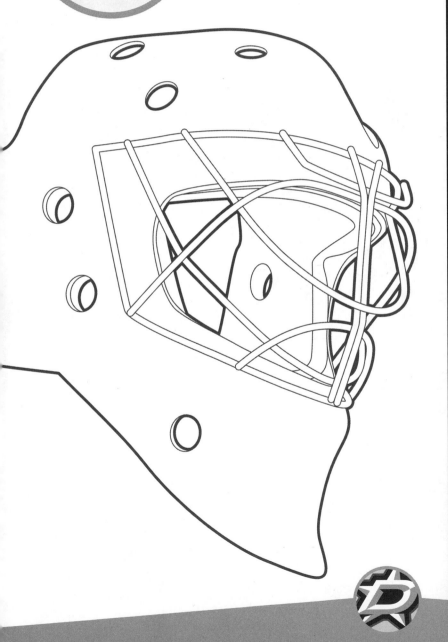

DRAW YOUR OWN MASK

QUIZ

HERE ARE NINE QUESTIONS TO SEE HOW MUCH YOU KNOW ABOUT THE STARS. GET SIX OR MORE RIGHT AND YOU'RE A STARTER. GET THREE OR LESS AND IT'S BACK TO THE MINORS!

1 Who's back as coach of the Stars?

2 He steered Dallas to its only Cup. Was that in 1999, 2001, 2003 or 2005?

3 Jason Spezza did more than play hockey as a kid. He won a baby contest and became a what?

4 Spezza was a pretty good hockey player, too, chosen second overall in 2001. Which team drafted him?

5 Another high-scoring Star was taken second overall by Boston in 2010. Who was that?

6 Only one Star has taken home the Art Ross Trophy as top scorer. Who is it?

7 Which former Star hoisted the Cup three times while with Chicago?

8 This Star went second overall, taken by the defunct Atlanta Thrashers in 2002. Who was it?

9 There's a Frenchman on the Dallas roster, too. He was born in Roubaix, which is close to the Belgian border. Can you name him?

WORD SEARCH

```
H A S I N P N O S B E E N
C A M F G H L S P R M I G
Q H J A M I E B E N N H R
F C I G S N L A Z G R C E
A S O T E D P E Z R U T B
K E D G C Y P R A H S I G
S V R M L H O O H V R R N
A A L K T U C L L E R F I
I E T O S C A O R B U L L
Y M A S A U E O C F M I K
B N E N O T H E L K N S W
H L N I A S I U H M A H S
C U J R N I N Z C A L J E
```

JAMIE BENN
HITCHCOCK
SHARP
SPEZZA
SEGUIN
ROUSSEL
RITCHIE
LEHTONEN
NIEMI
EAVES
KLINGBERG
SHORE
FAKSA
HAMHUIS

KARI LEHTONEN #32

FILL IN THE BLANKS

Hidden here is the last name of a current Dallas star. Find out who he is by filling in the blank spaces to get the nicknames of four NHL teams. We've given you the first and last letters of each team and one or two more to get you started. Once you've got them all, the Star's name will appear in the boxes reading from top to bottom.

S _ _ ☐ R _ _ S

I _ _ L _ _ N _ _ ☐ _ _ S

R _ _ D   W _ _ _ ☐ _ _ S

G _ _ L _ _ _ _ N   K ☐ _ _ G _ _ _ S

PUZZLE & QUIZ SOLUTIONS ON PAGE 195

BY THE NUMBERS

Ken Hitchcock is coaching in Dallas again, his second time with the Stars. In his first stint, he posted a regular season record of 277-154-72 and a playoff record of 47-33. How many games in total is that?

DYLAN
LARKIN
#71

DETROIT
RED WINGS

THE 2016-17 SEASON WAS ONE OF GOODBYES for the Detroit Red Wings, and the most touching farewell came on opening night.

Days before the 2015-16 ended, Red Wings legend Gordie Howe, one of the best and most universally beloved players in NHL history, passed away. Detroit used its home opener to pay teary-eyed tribute to the legend, looking back on some of the greatest moments from the man called Mr. Hockey. And eight months after Howe was celebrated, the Red Wings said another sad goodbye to one more longstanding member of their family, Mike Ilitch. He had owned the

franchise for 35 years, bringing four Stanley Cups to Detroit. That wasn't the last of the farewells, however.

The next was to Joe Louis Arena, the storied structure the Red Wings called home for 38 years. The famed building hosted six Stanley Cup finals and four championship teams.

And on the same night the Wings waved goodbye to their old stomping grounds, they did the same to their run of 25-straight playoff appearances. It was the longest streak in any major North American team sport, but few were surprised it ended in 2016-17. Goaltender Petr Mrazek's neck was nearly

sunburnt from the goal light, and the defense in front of the Red Wings' net couldn't stop a nosebleed. The offense wasn't helping, either. Only four teams scored fewer goals than Detroit, a far cry from the team's best days.

The Wings moved into their new home to start the 2017-18 season, and the hope is Detroit can return to its glory days with a youthful group that includes Dylan Larkin, Anthony Mantha and speedster Andreas Athanasiou. And if the kids are all right in 2017-18, the Wings might start another streak and say hello to their old friend, the playoffs, once again.

LEADERS

GOALS
TOMAS TATAR
25

ASSISTS
HENRIK ZETTERBERG
51

PENALTY MINUTES
STEVE OTT
63

ICE TIME
MIKE GREEN
23:33

GOALS-AGAINST AVERAGE
JIMMY HOWARD
2.10

SAVE PERCENTAGE
JIMMY HOWARD
.927

POINTS
HENRIK ZETTERBERG
68

PRESIDENT CHRISTOPHER ILITCH
GENERAL MANAGER KEN HOLLAND
COACH JEFF BLASHILL
MASCOT AL THE OCTOPUS

RECORD
33-36-13

HOME
17-17-7

AWAY
16-19-6

POINTS
79

GOALS FOR
198

GOALS AGAINST
244

AVERAGE AGE
28.4

ROOKIES
4

TOP
PROSPECT
EVGENY SVECHNIKOV
LW, 21,
ACQUIRED:
2015 DRAFT,
19TH OVERALL

HOME JERSEY

DRAW YOUR OWN MASK

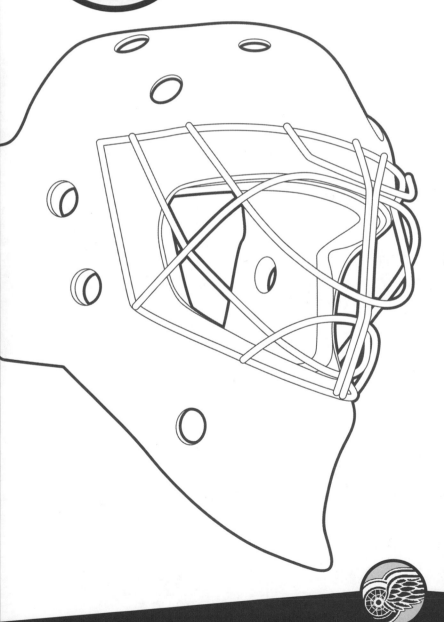

QUIZ

HERE ARE NINE QUESTIONS TO SEE HOW MUCH YOU KNOW ABOUT THE RED WINGS. GET SIX OR MORE RIGHT AND YOU'RE A STARTER. GET THREE OR LESS AND IT'S BACK TO THE MINORS!

1 What's 'The Joe'?

2 What's the name of the team's new arena?

3 In 2016-17, Detroit missed the playoffs for the first time in 20, 23, 25 or 27 straight years?

4 Henrik Zetterberg was so well thought of by the Red Wings that they signed him to the longest deal in team history in 2009. How many years was it for?

5 Frans Nielsen was the first player from what country to play in the NHL?

6 Dylan Larkin scored in his NHL debut while still a teenager, following in the footsteps of what great Red Wing (hint: he wore No. 19)?

7 Defenseman Xavier Ouellet is unique in that he was born in Basque Country in part of what nation?

8 Who was the Red Wings' coach before Jeff Blashill?

9 All three members of Detroit's famed 'Production Line' have had their jerseys retired by the Wings. Can you name at least two of them?

WORD SEARCH

```
A  T  H  A  N  A  S  I  O  U  T  A  Z
A  N  E  D  E  K  E  Y  S  E  R  J  E
B  T  G  N  A  R  C  B  L  A  B  X  Z
D  N  A  L  L  O  H  L  O  N  I  E  Z
E  P  E  M  R  N  K  A  K  Y  W  R  Z
L  A  A  A  O  W  M  S  N  Q  E  A  E
K  E  H  D  F  A  R  H  E  U  H  K  T
A  E  T  K  S  L  A  I  H  I  U  R  T
D  I  N  O  B  L  Z  L  C  S  A  L  R
E  U  A  A  H  Y  E  L  R  T  K  P  B
R  B  M  A  V  L  K  E  A  A  E  C  E
K  I  W  D  M  U  H  T  M  M  O  L  R
H  T  I  G  N  I  N  E  D  N  E  L  G
```

KRONWALL
HOLLAND
ZETTERBERG
BLASHILL
ABDELKADER
MRAZEK
NYQUIST
TATAR
MANTHA
GLENDENING
VANEK
ATHANASIOU
DEKEYSER
MARCHENKO

JIMMY HOWARD #35

FILL IN THE BLANKS

Hidden here is the last name of a current Red Wing star. Find out who he is by filling in the blank spaces to get the homes of 10 NHL teams, either the city or state they play in. We've given you the first and last letters of each city or state and one or two more to get you started. Once you've got them all, the Red Wing star's name will appear in the boxes reading from top to bottom.

```
A  _  _  _  □  O  _  _  A
W  _  _  N  N  _  _  _  _  □  G
E  _  _  M  _  _  _  _  □  _  _  N
M  _  _  _  _  N  E  _  _  _  _  □  A
L  _  _  S  V  □  _  _  _  _  S
D  _  _  T  □  _  _  _  _  T
C  _  _  L  _  _  _  _  □  _  S
M  _  _  N  _  _  _  _  □  _  _  L
T  _  _  □  _  _  N  _  _  O
C  _  _  _  _  □  A  _  Y
```

PUZZLE & QUIZ SOLUTIONS ON PAGE 195

BY THE NUMBERS

The Red Wings have retired seven numbers, including 5, 7, 9, 10, 12 and 19. If you add those up, you get the record number of wins posted by the Wings in a season (it's also an NHL record). How many was that?

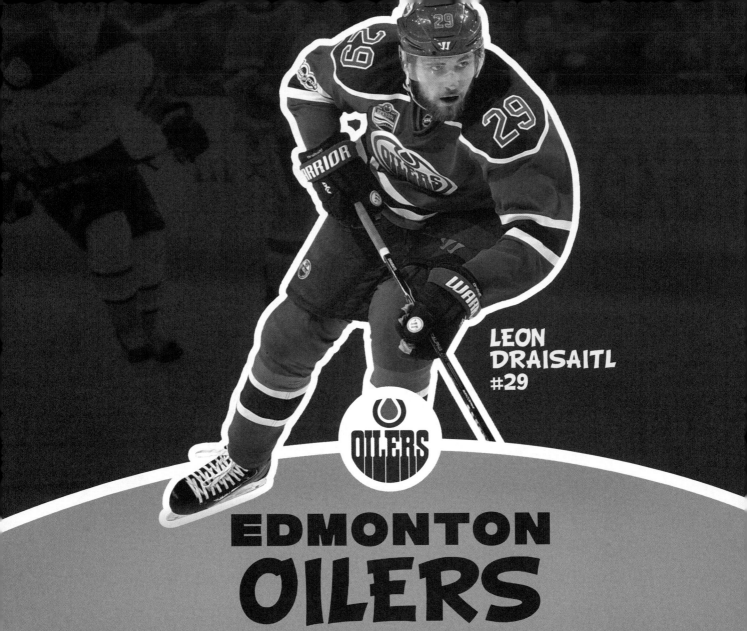

LEON DRAISAITL #29

EDMONTON OILERS

A DECADE OF DISAPPOINTMENT CAME TO AN end in Edmonton, and it was the can't-miss kid who led the way as Connor McDavid became the youngest captain in NHL history and took the Oilers back to the playoffs for the first time in 10 years.

McDavid, who missed half of his rookie season with an injury, was almost unstoppable in his second year in Edmonton. He was a human highlight reel, turning defensemen into pylons and making goaltenders consider changing jobs. McDavid pulled fans out of their seats with dazzling dekes, rocketed home shots that gave netminders whiplash and went end-to-end in a flash. He put

his speed on display at the All-Star Game, winning the fastest skater competition after completing a lap around the ice in just 13.3 seconds!

'Captain Connor' rightfully became 'King Connor' by the time the season ended, too. On the final day of the season, McDavid registered two assists to become the only player in the league to reach 100 points. That was enough for McDavid to take the throne as the season's scoring king just two years into his brilliant career.

There was more to the Oilers' explosion up the standings than McDavid, however. An eye-popping off-season trade saw Edmonton

swap Taylor Hall for Adam Larsson, who helped plug up a blueline that had been far too leaky in past seasons. Free agent signing Milan Lucic came in to be the Oilers' big rig, and while the monstrous left winger bashed opponents with his crushing checks, third-year center Leon Draisaitl tore up the scoring charts with a breakout season of his own. And Edmonton couldn't have made its way back to the playoffs without goaltender Cam Talbot, who set a franchise record with 42 wins.

The playoffs are only the first step for these exciting Oilers, though, and it might only be a matter of time before Connor and Co. have their Cup.

OILERS

LEADERS

GOALS
CONNOR MCDAVID
30

ASSISTS
CONNOR MCDAVID
70

PENALTY MINUTES
ZACK KASSIAN
101

ICE TIME
OSCAR KFLEBOM
22:22

GOALS-AGAINST AVERAGE
CAM TALBOT
2.39

SAVE PERCENTAGE
CAM TALBOT
.919

POINTS
CONNOR MCDAVID
100

PRESIDENT PETER CHIARELLI
GENERAL MANAGER PETER CHIARELLI
COACH TODD MCLELLAN
MASCOT HUNTER THE LYNX

RECORD
47-26-9

HOME
25-12-4

AWAY
22-14-5

POINTS
103

GOALS FOR
243

GOALS AGAINST
207

AVERAGE AGE
26.7

ROOKIES
4

TOP
PROSPECT
JESSE PULJUJARVI
RW, 19,
ACQUIRED:
2016 DRAFT,
4TH OVERALL

HOME JERSEY

OILERS

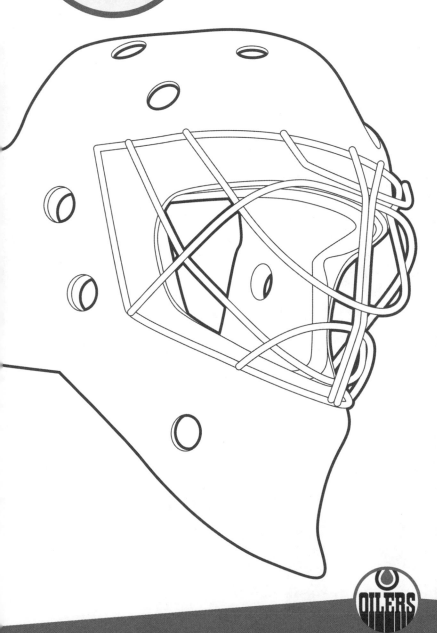

DRAW YOUR OWN MASK

OILERS

QUIZ

HERE ARE NINE QUESTIONS TO SEE HOW MUCH YOU KNOW ABOUT THE REVITALIZED OILERS. GET SIX OR MORE RIGHT AND YOU'RE A STARTER. GET THREE OR LESS AND IT'S BACK TO THE MINORS!

1 Rogers has given its name to the Oilers' new home and also to an arena in Vancouver as well as a ballpark in what city?

2 Leon Draisaitl had an unusual route to the NHL. Where did he play before coming to Canada?

3 Just like Wayne Gretzky, what trophy did Connor McDavid win in his second season?

4 McDavid is a big fan of another NHL superstar, a kid from Cole Harbour, N.S. Who's that?

5 Oilers coach Todd McLellan already has his name on the Stanley Cup, as he was an assistant with what Cup-winning team in 2008?

6 True or false? Cam Talbot was never drafted by an NHL team.

7 Milan Lucic is one tough customer. He's missed just 4, 6, 8 or 10 games the past four seasons combined?

8 Who did the Oilers take first overall in the 2011 draft?

9 The Oilers added to their D-corps when they acquired Adam Larsson in a trade for 2010's first-overall pick. Who was that?

WORD SEARCH

```
C D E Y S R E U M S T A A
T O B L A T M A C N M R C
I D E N R E I F L I E U K
N A R M O B F E L K C T I
N D L K G E K B E P D U L
A I E U E G C S N O R E L
L V Y B R A K L N H A R E
L A R S S O N O I T I F R
E D N T P E O Y S N S L A
L C X Z L R U H C E A R I
C M O G A P O O D G I J H
M I C M C U H N L U T L C
U L G R E T Z K Y N L N H
```

MCLELLAN
EBERLE
LUCIC
MCDAVID
NUGENT-HOPKINS
ROGERS PLACE
CAM TALBOT
GRETZKY
MAROON
KLEFBOM
SEKERA
DRAISAITL
LARSSON
CHIARELLI

CAM TALBOT #33

FILL IN THE BLANKS

Hidden here is the last name of a current Oiler star. Find out who he is by filling in the blank spaces to get the homes of seven NHL teams, either the city or state they play in. We've given you the first and last letters of each city or state and one or two more to get you started. Once you've got them all, the Oiler star's lastname will appear in the boxes reading from top to bottom.

T _ _ ☐ _ A B _ _ Y
V _ _ _ ☐ _ U _ _ R
E ☐ _ _ O _ _ _ _ N
D _ _ _ L ☐ S
N _ _ _ H ☐ _ _ _ _ E
A _ _ ☐ Z _ _ _ A
F _ _ _ _ I ☐ A

PUZZLE & QUIZ SOLUTIONS ON PAGE 195

BY THE NUMBERS

Last season, Connor McDavid became the first Oiler to win the Art Ross Trophy since Wayne Gretzky won his last with Edmonton in 1987. How many years separated those two Oiler wins?

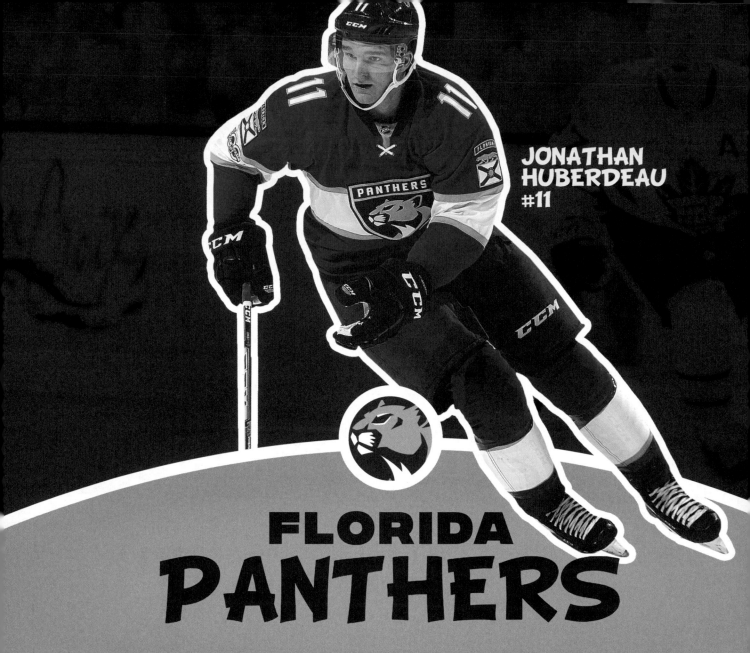

JONATHAN
HUBERDEAU
#11

FLORIDA PANTHERS

THE FLORIDA PANTHERS HAD THEIR BEST season in franchise history in 2015-16 , pairing youthful skill with veteran smarts to build a fast, ferocious squad that was fun to watch. But those powerful Cats performed more like puny kittens in 2016-17, following up their best year with one the teams can't wait to forget.

Things were cloudy in the Sunshine State both on and off the ice, and the signs of a tough season were there before the Panthers could even begin. Flashy winger Jonathan Huberdeau was set to be the star attacker coming off the best season of his career, but he suffered an ankle injury during the final game of the pre-season that put him out of action for more than half of the year. Huberdeau's injury alone would have been bad enough, but there weren't enough Band-Aids in the world to keep the bruised and battered Panthers together. Everyone from veteran goaltender Roberto Luongo to surprising scorer Jonathan Marchessault missed time, and when gifted center Aleksander Barkov went down with a back injury, it seemed like Florida had been cursed.

There was at least some excitement surrounding the Panthers as Jaromir Jagr, scored his way up the career points list. The 45-year-old legend recorded his 1,888th point to move into second on the all-time list behind Wayne Gretzky. Jagr finished the season with 1,914 points in his incredible 23-year career and became only the fourth player in league history to play 1,700 games.

But overall the campaign was disappointing for a hopeful Panthers team. As coach Gerard Gallant worked his hardest to piece together a patchwork Panthers squad, Florida struggled to put up points and Gallant was shockingly fired. Sending GM Tom Rowe behind the Panthers bench didn't put any spring in the Cats' step, however, and there was no clawing back into playoff position once Florida had fallen out.

FLORIDA

LEADERS

POINTS
VINCENT TROCHECK
54 →

GOALS
JONATHAN MARCHESSAULT
30

ASSISTS
KIETH YANDLE
36

PENALTY MINUTES
ALEX PETROVIC
79

ICE TIME
KEITH YANDLE
22:02

GOALS-AGAINST AVERAGE
JAMES REIMER
2.53

SAVE PERCENTAGE
JAMES REIMER
.920

PRESIDENT MATTHEW CALDWELL
GENERAL MANAGER DALE TALLON
COACH BOB BOUGHNER
MASCOT STANLEY C. PANTHER

RECORD
35-36-11

HOME
19-19-3

AWAY
16-17-8

POINTS
81

GOALS FOR
205

GOALS AGAINST
231

AVERAGE AGE
28.6

ROOKIES
4

TOP
PROSPECT
OWEN TIPPETT
RW, 18,
ACQUIRED:
2017 DRAFT,
10TH OVERALL

HOME JERSEY

DRAW YOUR OWN MASK

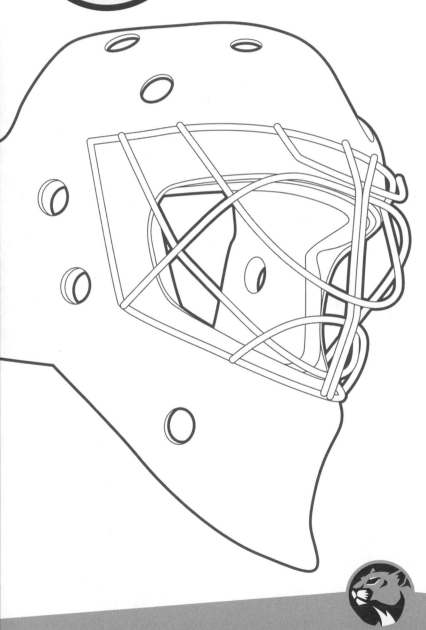

QUIZ

HERE ARE NINE QUESTIONS TO SEE HOW MUCH YOU KNOW ABOUT THE PANTHERS. GET SIX OR MORE RIGHT AND YOU'RE A STARTER. GET THREE OR LESS AND IT'S BACK TO THE MINORS!

1 The Panthers are based in Florida, in a suburb of what city?

2 Who took over as Panthers coach in late November last season?

3 Jonathan Marchessault previously played with what other Florida-based team?

4 What Panther was chosen first overall in the 2014 draft?

5 Keith Yandle played over 400 consecutive games with what team?

6 James Reimer was a big fan of this team as a boy and then went on to play six seasons with them. Which team was it?

7 Jaromir Jagr turned how old in mid-February of 2017?

8 Jussi Jokinen is a specialist in what part of the game?

9 Whose nickname is 'Bobby Lou?'

WORD SEARCH

```
M T K L N E N I K O J R Z
A N R U E R A C A T S E G
S Q E O A M E B L I B T N
E L M N L H O L E N I N O
I C I G C D A L B K E E S
Y A E O O W G S Y Q E C E
M A R C H E S S A U L T H
S T N K O D Y N R I R & T
R I D D B P A O C S E B A
E U N A L E W L R T M B M
M E I Z N E K C A M I E W
E I W E K U B O Z C Y E K
D T R G A J R I M O R A J
```

EKBLAD
ROWE
MACKENZIE
JOKINEN
BB&T CENTER
YANDLE
MARCHESSAULT
REIMER
TROCHECK
PYSYK
JAROMIR JAGR
MATHESON
DEMERS
LUONGO

JAMES REIMER #34

FILL IN THE BLANKS

Hidden here is the last name of a current Panther star. Find out who he is by filling in the blank spaces to get the nicknames of six NHL teams. We've given you the first and last letters of each team and one or two more to get you started. Once you've got them all, the Panther star's name will appear in the boxes reading from top to bottom.

D ☐ _ _ I _ S

C _ _ N _ _ _ _ ☐ S

S _ _ ☐ R _ S

I _ ☐ _ _ N _ E _ S

C _ P _ _ _ ☐ S

C _ _ N _ _ ☐ _ E _ S

PUZZLE & QUIZ SOLUTIONS ON PAGE 196

BY THE NUMBERS

Jaromir Jagr is a wonder, still going strong at age 45. He's also the all-time leader in game-winning goals with 135. That's exactly how many times his age?

ANZE
KOPITAR
#11

LOS ANGELES
KINGS

THE STANLEY CUP IS THE NHL'S CROWN JEWEL, and the Kings have taken league's throne twice in the past six years. However, L.A.'s style of play left the once mighty franchise looking like anything but royalty as the Kings missed the playoffs for the second time in three seasons.

The biggest problem with Hollywood's team as the Kings fell short of the post-season was that there was no glitz or glamor to their offense. New captain Anze Kopitar, for instance, was still a defensive dynamo, but the Slovenian center fired home only 12 goals all year. Meanwhile, five-time 20-goal scor-

er Dustin Brown only found twine 14 times and former 40-goal scorer Marian Gaborik managed a measly 10 goals. Once the biggest, baddest squad in the league, it became clear as the season wore on that L.A. was no longer able to bully its speedier, more skilled opponents, and when the season ended, only five teams had scored fewer goals than the Kings.

If there was ever a season Los Angeles could have used some offensive firepower, 2016-17 was it. On opening night, brick wall goaltender Jonathan Quick was lost to a groin injury. With Quick out, veteran backup Peter Budaj stonewalled the opposition as best he

could behind a strong Kings blueline that included Jake Muzzin, Alec Martinez and 2016 Norris Trophy winner, Drew Doughty.

In the end, though, it wasn't enough. There were still too many cracks in the Kings' fortress, and missing the playoffs meant changes were coming. Longtime GM Dean Lombardi and coach Darryl Sutter were fired, and one of the league's oldest rosters was in for an injection of youth before 2017-18. Now that the Kings have made some tweaks and adjustments, the hope in Los Angeles is that they will be crowned league champions once again.

LEADERS

GOALS
JEFF CARTER
32

ASSISTS
ANZE KOPITAR
40

PENALTY MINUTES
KYLE CLIFFORD
92

ICE TIME
DREW DOUGHTY
27:08

GOALS-AGAINST AVERAGE
PETER BUDAJ
2.12

SAVE PERCENTAGE
PETER BUDAJ
.917

POINTS
JEFF CARTER
66

PRESIDENT DAN BECKERMAN
GENERAL MANAGER ROB BLAKE
COACH JOHN STEVENS
MASCOT BAILEY

RECORD
39-35-8

HOME
23-16-2

AWAY
16-19-2

POINTS
86

GOALS FOR
199

GOALS AGAINST
201

AVERAGE AGE
29.1

ROOKIES
2

TOP PROSPECT
GABE VILARDI
C, 18,
ACQUIRED:
2017 DRAFT,
11TH OVERALL

HOME JERSEY

DRAW YOUR OWN MASK

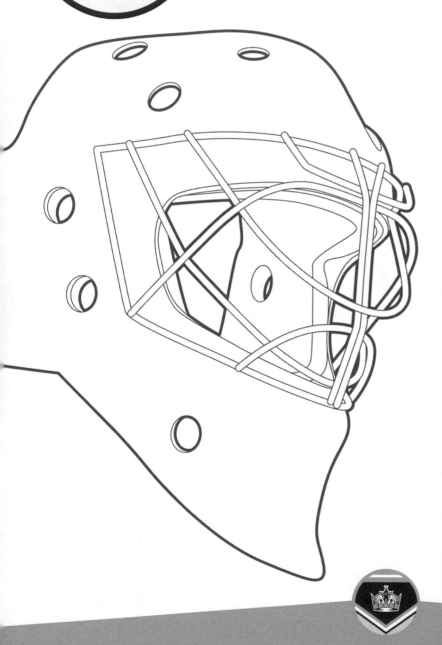

QUIZ

HERE ARE NINE QUESTIONS TO SEE HOW MUCH YOU KNOW ABOUT THE L.A.-BASED KINGS. GET SIX OR MORE RIGHT AND YOU'RE A STARTER. GET THREE OR LESS AND IT'S BACK TO THE MINORS!

1 After a disappointing season, the Kings fired coach Darryl Sutter. He had led them to how many Stanley Cups?

2 Los Angeles traded for a goalie late in the season and then traded him after the season ended. Who is he?

3 The goaltender in the previous question is tall, the tallest ever to play his position. How tall is he?

4 Do you remember who was named the Conn Smythe Trophy winner when the Kings hoisted their first Cup in 2012?

5 Jeff Carter led the Kings in scoring last season. He's been around, having played for two other NHL teams. Can you name them?

6 Jarome Iginla has travelled, too, but is best known for his long stint as captain of what team?

7 Wearing the 'C' in L.A. is Anze Kopitar. That's an exotic name. Where is he from?

8 Many NHL arenas are also home to an NBA team, but the Staples Center has two. Can you name them both??

9 Durable Trevor Lewis, who played all 82 games last season, is from this 2002 Olympic host city. What city (hint: it's in the U.S.)?

WORD SEARCH

```
Q M P Y A T R G M Y T A N
L U E O L U J A T R M R I
J Z I T H E C H L N F C C
E Z B C S S G A B O R I K
F I E R K U I A R S W L S
F N V A O Y D B N R E O H
C E I D P W O H A A H F O
A S N K I R N E I E U F R
R I N O T S O R S P P O E
T U V V A Y U H C S K T T
E B E D R O F F I L C S R
R E T N E C S E L P A T S
C T I P A D I M B E N T Q
```

KOPITAR
CLIFFORD
JEFF CARTER
DOUGHTY
STAPLES CENTER
FORBORT
QUICK
PEARSON
BROWN
TOFFOLI
GABORIK
NICK SHORE
BISHOP
MUZZIN

JONATHAN QUICK #32

FILL IN THE BLANKS

Hidden here is the last name of a current King star. Find out who he is by filling in the blank spaces to get the homes of five NHL teams, either the city or state they play in. We've given you the first and last letters of each city or state and one or two more to get you started. Once you've got them all, the King star's name will appear in the boxes reading from top to bottom.

C _ L _ _ _ ☐ _ S

A ☐ _ _ Z _ _ _ A

B _ _ _ _ T ☐ N

N _ _ ☐ Y _ _ _ K

T _ _ R _ ☐ _ O

PUZZLE & QUIZ SOLUTIONS ON PAGE 196

BY THE NUMBERS

L.A.'s Drew Doughty led the NHL in shifts per game last season, averaging a whopping 32. If a shift lasts a minute, how much time did he spend on the bench each game (assuming no overtime)?

ZACH
PARISE
#11

MINNESOTA
WILD

COACH BRUCE BOUDREAU WAS BROUGHT aboard to make the Minnesota Wild better. What no one expected, though, is that one season under Boudreau could turn them from a Western Conference pretender into one of the NHL's top contenders.

Boudreau's bunch came storming out of the gate to start the season, winning six of their first nine games, but it was the streak that started in late-November that allowed Minnesotans to scream from the rooftops that their team was here to make some noise. What started with a victory over the Edmonton Oilers continued into 12-game winning

streak, pushing the Wild to the top of the Central Division and sending Minnesota into a state of pure joy.

The team was led by goaltender Devan Dubnyk, who shut down opposing snipers with incredible play in the first half of the season. His job was made much easier thanks to a sturdy defense that was guided by marathon man Ryan Suter, master blaster Jared Spurgeon and booming bodychecker Matthew Dumba.

Meanwhile, it was tough to find a team in the league that had more weapons up front than Minnesota. Mikael Granlund estab-

lished himself as a scoring stud with a breakout season, Nino Niederreiter skated his way to success and veteran Eric Staal turned back the clock, looking like his old self with a near 30-goal season. That's not to mention the standout play of captain Mikko Koivu, who was again the rock the Wild relied on when they needed it most.

By the time the season had ended, Minnesota had slipped to second in the West, but it was still cause for celebration. And after the best season in franchise history, the Wild appear to be on the road to turning the Twin Cities into Title Town.

LEADERS

POINTS
MIKAEL GRANLUND
69

GOALS
ERIC STAAL
28

ASSISTS
MIKAEL GRANLUND
43

PENALTY MINUTES
CHRIS STEWART
94

ICE TIME
RYAN SUTER
26:55

GOALS-AGAINST AVERAGE
DEVAN DUBNYK
2.25

SAVE PERCENTAGE
DEVAN DUBNYK
.923

PRESIDENT MATT MAJKA
GENERAL MANAGER CHUCK FLETCHER
COACH BRUCE BOUDREAU
MASCOT NORDY

RECORD
49-25-8

HOME
27-12-2

AWAY
22-13-2

POINTS
106

GOALS FOR
263

GOALS AGAINST
206

AVERAGE AGE
28.3

ROOKIES
1

TOP
PROSPECT
JOEL
ERIKSSON EK
C, 20,
ACQUIRED:
2015 DRAFT,
20TH OVERALL

HOME JERSEY

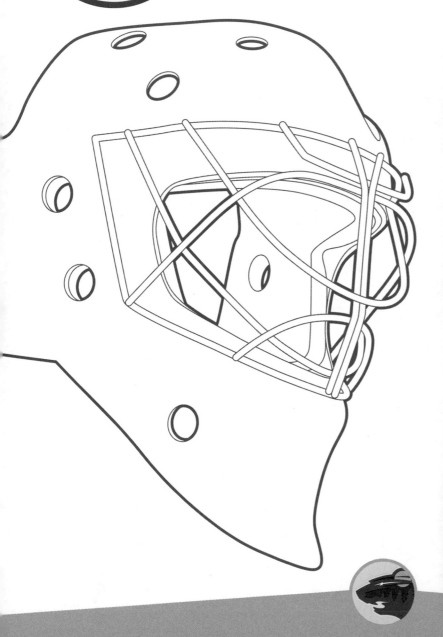

DRAW YOUR OWN MASK

QUIZ

HERE ARE NINE QUESTIONS TO SEE HOW MUCH YOU KNOW ABOUT THE WILD. GET SIX OR MORE RIGHT AND YOU'RE A STARTER. GET THREE OR LESS AND IT'S BACK TO THE MINORS!

1 Bruce Boudreau has never been shy about expressing himself, hence his nickname. What is it?

2 As captain, Mikko Koivu helped what country to gold at the 2011 World Championship?

3 Eric is the oldest of the four hockey-playing Staal brothers. Can you name the other three?

4 Eric previously won a Stanley Cup with what team?

5 Nino Niederreiter was drafted fifth, sixth or seventh overall in 2010?

6 Zach Parise has been both alternate captain and captain in two Olympic Games, winning one medal. What color was it?

7 Devan Dubnyk won a trophy in 2015 not usually given to goalies. Which was it?

8 True or false? Ryan Suter's father, Bob, was with the famed Miracle on Ice team in 1980.

9 Jason Pominville previously captained what Atlantic Division team?

WORD SEARCH

```
R  X  C  E  L  E  N  E  R  G  Y  G  E
E  D  N  T  I  H  C  S  E  K  M  R  L
T  T  E  S  A  V  I  H  T  M  I  A  L
I  I  R  T  E  D  J  R  U  C  S  N  I
E  N  O  E  G  R  U  P  S  Y  E  L  V
R  P  F  W  S  U  D  T  N  W  K  U  N
R  E  Y  A  O  I  A  A  A  M  R  N  I
E  T  E  R  M  A  R  E  Y  B  E  D  M
D  D  N  T  L  I  M  A  R  S  K  O  O
E  U  T  N  O  I  G  L  P  D  C  V  P
I  M  I  K  K  O  K  O  I  V  U  D  R
N  B  C  D  V  U  D  Q  N  G  Z  O  H
L  A  I  E  H  K  Y  N  B  U  D  I  B
```

GRANLUND
ERIC STAAL
BOUDREAU
STEWART
RYAN SUTER
ZUCKER
DUBNYK
MIKKO KOIVU
PARISE
XCEL ENERGY
POMINVILLE
SPURGEON
DUMBA
NIEDERREITER

DEVAN DUBNYK #40

FILL IN THE BLANKS

Hidden here is the last name of a current Wild star. Find out who he is by filling in the blank spaces to get the nicknames of six NHL teams. We've given you the first and last letters of each team and one or two more to get you started. Once you've got them all, the Wild star's name will appear in the boxes reading from top to bottom.

I __ L __ N ☐ ___ S

B __ ☐ __ N S

S __ ☐ R __ S

A _____ A ☐ ____ E

F __ ☐ E __ S

G ___ D __ N ☐ ___ G ___ S

PUZZLE & QUIZ SOLUTIONS ON PAGE 196

BY THE NUMBERS

The Wild's Ryan Suter and Jason Zucker were tied for the best plus-minus in the league last season. They both finished plus-34. But that was a far cry from the record established by Bobby Orr in 1970-71, when he finished plus-124. So, Orr was how much better than Suter and Zucker?

ALEX GALCHENYUK #27

MONTREAL CANADIENS

AS 24-TIME STANLEY CUP CHAMPIONS, IT'S safe to say that winning isn't everything in Montreal – it's the only thing. So, when the Canadiens failed to make the playoffs in 2015-16, it was a sign that changes were coming, but the biggest change Montreal made left jaws on the floor and eyes popping out of their sockets.

After a disappointing season, Montreal decided that an attitude adjustment was required. That meant bringing in feisty competitors and becoming the type of team that could win with skill or sandpaper. In a move that shocked the hockey world twice over, that meant trading P.K. Subban, one

of the most fun-loving and fun-to-watch defensemen in the league, for Nashville Predators captain Shea Weber, a hulking mass of a blueliner who can rip slapshots at light speed and crush attacking forwards into dust.

In the early part of the season, the trade left Canadiens GM Marc Bergevin looking like Albert Einstein. He had come up with the winning the formula, it seemed, with Weber coming in to patch any holes in Montreal's leaky defense to protect Carey Price, the Canadiens' can't-beat keeper.

But by mid-season, however, Montreal was starting to slide. Price didn't look like

himself, the once-solid defense was falling apart piece by piece and the offense, which had been led to success early on by captain Max Pacioretty, Alex Galchenyuk and newcomer Alexander Radulov, had stalled. So, out of nowhere, coach Michel Therrien was fired and replaced in an instant by Claude Julien, who had just been let go by the rival Boston Bruins.

With the hiring of Julien, Bergevin's design for the Bleu, Blanc et Rouge appears nearly complete, but the Canadiens, and their fans, won't be satisfied with Bergevin's work until the Stanley Cup comes back to Montreal.

LEADERS

GOALS
MAX PACIORETTY
35

ASSISTS
ALEXANDER RADULOV
36

PENALTY MINUTES
ANDREW SHAW
110

ICE TIME
SHEA WEBER
25:03

GOALS-AGAINST AVERAGE
CAREY PRICE
2.23

SAVE PERCENTAGE
CAREY PRICE
.923

POINTS
MAX PACIORETTY
67

PRESIDENT GEOFF MOLSON
GENERAL MANAGER MARC BERGEVIN
COACH CLAUDE JULIEN
MASCOT YOUPPI!

RECORD
47-26-9

HOME
24-12-5

AWAY
23-14-4

POINTS
103

GOALS FOR
223

GOALS AGAINST
198

AVERAGE AGE
28.8

ROOKIES
3

TOP
PROSPECT
NOAH JUULSEN
D, 20,
ACQUIRED:
2015 DRAFT,
26TH OVERALL

HOME JERSEY

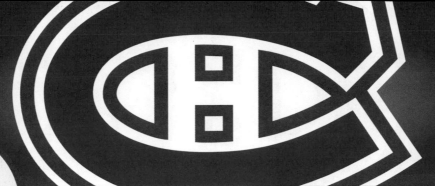

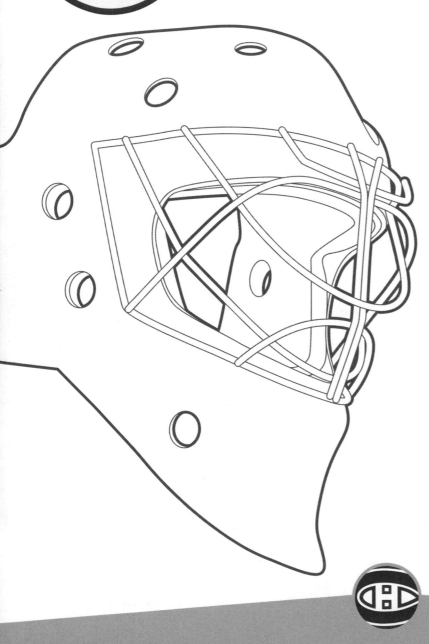

DRAW YOUR OWN MASK

HERE ARE NINE QUESTIONS TO SEE HOW MUCH YOU KNOW ABOUT THE HIGH-FLYING CANADIENS. GET SIX OR MORE RIGHT AND YOU'RE A STARTER. GET THREE OR LESS AND IT'S BACK TO THE MINORS!

1 The Canadiens have won two dozen Cups over the years. That's how many?

2 Who succeeded Michel Therrien as coach on Valentine's Day (no love for Michel!)?

3 Max Pacioretty can put points on the board, but he's only received one trophy in his years with Montreal. Which is it?

4 Montreal took Guy Lafleur with the first pick of the 1971 draft. How many times have the Canadiens selected first overall since?

5 The Bell Centre has seating for just over 18,000 19,000, 20,000 or 21,000 people?

6 Rocket Richard dazzled fans, becoming hockey's first 500-goal man. What was his real first name?

7 How many games did Carey Price win to start to the 2016-17 season?

8 Who did the Habs trade to get Shea Weber?

9 Jeff Petry's dad was also a professional athlete. What was his sport?

WORD SEARCH

```
S  P  B  Y  A  T  R  G  M  Q  T  A  M
L  N  E  I  L  U  J  A  E  R  M  R  I
A  E  R  T  N  G  C  L  X  E  B  C  T
E  A  G  A  R  D  D  L  R  B  I  E  C
C  P  E  M  R  Y  K  A  C  E  W  N  H
I  A  V  A  O  S  D  G  N  W  E  A  E
R  E  I  R  N  U  K  H  A  A  H  K  L
P  S  N  K  L  N  M  E  I  E  U  E  L
Y  I  N  O  B  S  O  R  S  H  P  L  Q
E  U  V  V  H  Y  U  H  C  S  K  P  T
R  B  E  A  U  L  I  E  U  A  E  C  R
A  I  W  D  M  U  H  N  L  M  O  L  O
C  T  I  P  A  C  I  O  R  E  T  T  Y
```

BERGEVIN
PACIORETTY
JULIEN
MITCHELL
RADULOV
SHAW
CAREY PRICE
MARKOV
SHEA WEBER
PLEKANEC
GALLAGHER
BEAULIEU
PETRY
DANAULT

CAREY PRICE #31

FILL IN THE BLANKS

Hidden here is the last name of a current Canadien star. Find out who he is by filling in the blank spaces to get the homes of 10 NHL teams, either the city or state they play in. We've given you the first and last letters of each city or state and one or two more to get you started. Once you've got them all, the Canadien star's name will appear in the boxes reading from top to bottom.

```
P __ I L _____ □ ___ A
L □ S  V _____ S
C ___ □ A __ O
W __ N N □ ____ G
E __ M □ _____ N
D __ T □ ___ T
M __ N ____ □ __ L
T __ R ____ □ O
O T □ ____ A
N __ W  □ O __ K
```

PUZZLE & QUIZ SOLUTIONS ON PAGE 196

BY THE NUMBERS

The Montreal Canadiens have retired a whopping 15 numbers. Among them are 1, 2, 5, 9 and 16. Add those up and you get their highest retired number. What number is that and who wore it (hint: it was a goalie)?

P.K.
SUBBAN
#76

NASHVILLE PREDATORS

DOWN IN NASHVILLE, KNOWN AS MUSIC CITY, the only songs that had been sung over the past several seasons were those of playoff heartbreak. So, with a plan to take the franchise to another level, GM David Poile hit the trade market and dealt the Predators' captain in hopes his band would start singing a different tune.

The Shea Weber trade changed the face of the franchise. Weber had led the Predators for more than 10 years and was the cornerstone of the Smashville style that had made the team successful during his time in Tennessee. After recent playoff failures, though, Nashville decided it was time for a new look – more speed, more skill and more style – and that meant trading Weber to the Montreal Canadiens for flashy defender P.K. Subban.

Subban's addition to the blueline made an already deadly defense all the more lethal, too. Underrated star Roman Josi stepped his game up even further, power play specialist Ryan Ellis ripped home a career-best 16 goals and Mattias Ekholm logged major minutes as the steady shutdown guy.

Don't go thinking Nashville was all defense, though.

Filip Forsberg used his superhuman shot to bulge twine all season long, firing pucks with deadeye aim and blink-and-you'll-miss-it quickness. During one five-game stretch, Forsberg scored 10 goals, including back-to-back hat tricks! He wasn't alone in lighting lamps, however, as the brilliant breakout of Viktor Arvidsson gave Nashville two top offensive weapons. Arvidsson jumped from the fourth line to the first, carving out a place alongside Forsberg and center Ryan Johansen, and the trio sank their teeth into the scoresheet on a nightly basis.

And when the post-season rolled around, Nashville danced all the way to the Stanley Cup final for the first time in franchise history.

LEADERS

POINTS
VIKTOR ARVIDSSON
61

GOALS
VIKTOR ARVIDSSON
31

ASSISTS
RYAN JOHANSEN
47

PENALTY MINUTES
AUSTIN WATSON
99

ICE TIME
ROMAN JOSI
25:04

GOALS-AGAINST AVERAGE
JUUSE SAROS
2.35

SAVE PERCENTAGE
JUUSE SAROS
.923

PRESIDENT SEAN HENRY
GENERAL MANAGER DAVID POILE
COACH PETER LAVIOLETTE
MASCOT GNASH

RECORD
41-29-12

HOME
24-9-8

AWAY
17-20-4

POINTS
94

GOALS FOR
238

GOALS AGAINST
220

AVERAGE AGE
27.9

ROOKIES
1

TOP PROSPECT
DANTE FABBRO
D, 19,
ACQUIRED:
2016 DRAFT,
17TH OVERALL

HOME JERSEY

DRAW
YOUR OWN
MASK

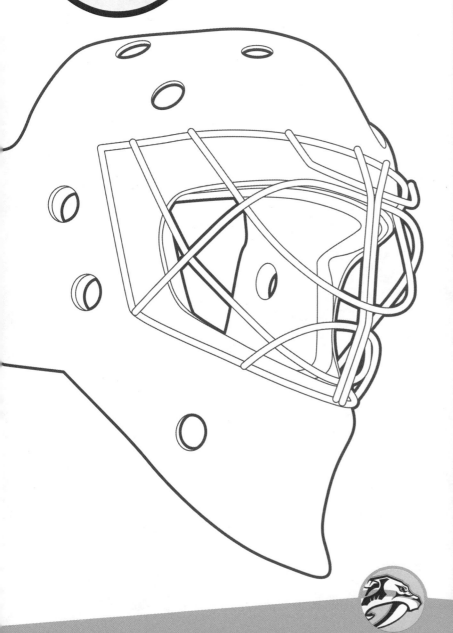

QUIZ

HERE ARE NINE QUESTIONS TO SEE HOW MUCH YOU KNOW ABOUT THE PREDS. GET SIX OR MORE RIGHT AND YOU'RE A STARTER. GET THREE OR LESS AND IT'S BACK TO THE MINORS!

1 The city of Nashville is known by what nickname?

2 Sniper Filip Forsberg was a first-round pick of what team (not the Preds)?

3 Coach Peter Laviolette won a Stanley Cup with what team in 2006?

4 Laviolette then coached what team before landing in Nashville?

5 Who preceded now retired Mike Fisher as captain of the Predators?

6 Fisher is married to what famous country music singer?

7 Alternate captain Roman Josi hails from what Swiss city, famous for its bear pit?

8 Ex-Pred James Neal, led the league in what scoring stat while with Pittsburgh in 2011-12 (hint: he got 18)?

9 Ryan Johansen not only played in the 2015 All-Star Game, he also earned what honor?

WORD SEARCH

```
B T J L N K E E W O S R N
A L R A E P N M L O H K E
Z A E O M N O B L I R T S
E V M N I E T I E N Y T N
N I I R K D S L L K A E A
O O E O E G E N Y E N C H
S L R C F R G S E U E N O
S E N K I E D N R A L A J
D T O D S B I O C S L B A
I T N A H S R S R T I B M
V E I Z E R B T A M S U W
R I W E R O M A N J O S I
A T R G A F R W M E G A J
```

ROMAN JOSI
MIKE FISHER
LAVIOLETTE
POILE
JAMES NEAL
BRIDGESTONE
FORSBERG
ARVIDSSON
JOHANSEN
WATSON
RYAN ELLIS
RINNE
SUBBAN
EKHOLM

PEKKA RINNE #35

FILL IN THE BLANKS

Hidden here is the last name of a recently retired Predator star. Find out who he is by filling in the blank spaces to get the nicknames of six NHL teams. We've given you a bunch of letters to get you started. Once you've got them all, the Predator star's name will appear in the boxes reading from top to bottom.

☐ _ _ Y _ _ _ S

R _ _ D W ☐ _ _ _ S

I ☐ _ _ A N _ _ _ _ _ S

B _ _ _ _ _ K ☐ A _ _ _ S

R _ _ _ G ☐ _ S

S _ _ A ☐ S

PUZZLE & QUIZ SOLUTIONS ON PAGE 196

BY THE NUMBERS

Nashville was a threat even when a man down last season, as the Predators scored a league-leading 12 shorthanded goals. They finished a mere +16 in goal differential (240 for, 224 against), so those 12 goals made up what percent of their differential?

KYLE
PALMIERI
#21

NEW JERSEY
DEVILS

GONE ARE THE GLORY DAYS OF YOUNG Martin Brodeur, Scott Stevens and Co. in New Jersey, and even the near-championship era that included Zach Parise, Ilya Kovalchuk and veteran Martin Brodeur has come and passed. These are the dark days for the Devils.

It's not that GM Ray Shero didn't try to light a fire under his team, however. In the off-season, Shero saw the chance to ignite his roster, so he pulled off a masterpiece trade, sending defenseman Adam Larsson to the Edmonton Oilers and bringing 2010 first-overall pick Taylor Hall to New Jersey. A speed demon gifted with highlight-reel talent, Hall dazzled and delighted with his

scoring touch, giving the Devils a welcome addition to what had been an awful offense the year prior.

But adding Hall alone couldn't help the Devils outrun their dreadful defense. The blueline was patched together with pieces that were too inexperienced, too slow or too overpowered, and no amount of mixing and matching could help the ragtag group keep pucks out of the New Jersey net. Not even Cory Schneider, one of the league's best goaltenders, could fight off the ridiculous amount of rubber he faced. Be it tired, overworked or simply outmatched, Schneider had his worst year as a Devil, trying but ul-

timately failing to get New Jersey out of the league's basement.

When the Devils did finally have something to celebrate, it was the farewell to a familiar face. After more than 1,200 games in New Jersey, Patrik Elias called it a career, finishing his time in the NHL as the franchise's all-time leader in goals and points.

While the Devils said goodbye to one great, they said hello to potentially another. New Jersey won the draft lottery and took Nico Hischier with the first-overall pick in the 2017 draft. Hischier gives Devils fans hope for a new stick-wielding savior and the chance for New Jersey to grow another winner.

LEADERS

POINTS
TAYLOR HALL
53

GOALS
KYLE PALMIERI
26
—
ASSISTS
TAYLOR HALL
33
—
PENALTY MINUTES
MILES WOOD
86
—
ICE TIME
ANDY GREENE
21:56
—
GOALS-AGAINST AVERAGE
KEITH KINKAID
2.64
—
SAVE PERCENTAGE
KEITH KINCAID
.916

PRESIDENT HUGH WEBER
GENERAL MANAGER RAY SHERO
COACH JOHN HYNES
MASCOT NJ DEVIL

RECORD
28-40-14

HOME
16-17-8

AWAY
12-23-6

POINTS
70

GOALS FOR
180

GOALS AGAINST
241

AVERAGE AGE
28.1

ROOKIES
5

TOP
PROSPECT
NICO HISCHIER
C, 18,
ACQUIRED:
2017 DRAFT,
1ST OVERALL

HOME JERSEY

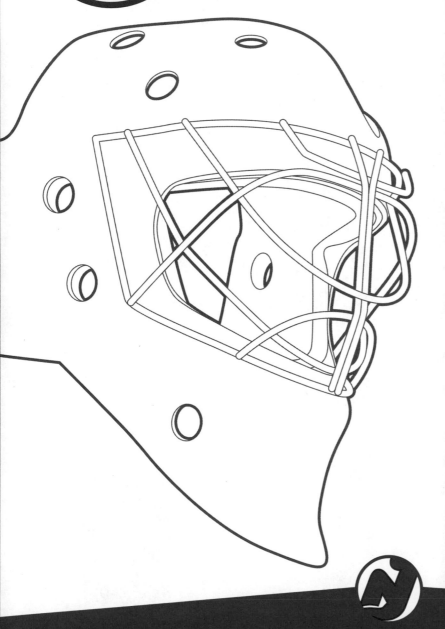

DRAW YOUR OWN MASK

QUIZ

HERE ARE NINE QUESTIONS TO SEE HOW MUCH YOU KNOW ABOUT THE DEVILS. GET SIX OR MORE RIGHT AND YOU'RE A STARTER. GET THREE OR LESS AND IT'S BACK TO THE MINORS!

1 GM Ray Shero is the son of what Hall of Fame coach?

2 Who did he succeed as GM?

3 In college, ex-Devil Mike Cammalleri played in a game that attracted some 74,000 fans and was dubbed The Cold War. It was between his school – Michigan – and what rival?

4 Taylor Hall was taken first, second or third overall in the 2010 draft?

5 What Hall of Fame goalie did Cory Schneider replace in New Jersey?

6 Stefan Noesen was born in Plano, Texas, which is also the birthplace of what disgraced cyclist?

7 Ben Lovejoy is nicknamed 'The Reverend' after what Simpson's character?

8 Which Devil played with the Devils Youth Hockey Club?

9 Who did Andy Greene succeed as captain of the Devils?

WORD SEARCH

```
S Z P Y W T N G R Y G A N
L L A H R O L Y A T R R I
J A I C E E O H Y N E S R
E I B S H S G D S O E I E
R T E R E A I A H S N L D
W N V A O V D B E R E O I
C E I G P H E N R I Q U E
O D N K I R N R O E U F N
R U N O T S O C S P P O H
I R E I M L A P C O K T C
E P E D R J F D I L N S S
C A M M A L L E R I A T S
A T I Z O D I R B U N O Y
```

GREENE
HYNES
ZAJAC
HENRIQUE
CAMMALLERI
PALMIERI
PRUDENTIAL
TAYLOR HALL
WOOD
NOESEN
SCHNEIDER
RAY SHERO
SEVERSON
ZACHA

CORY SCHNEIDER #35

PUZZLE & QUIZ SOLUTIONS ON PAGE 196

FILL IN THE BLANKS

Hidden here is the last name of a current Devil star. Find out who he is by filling in the blank spaces to get the homes of six NHL teams, either the city or state they play in. We've given you a bunch of letters to get you started. Once you've got them all, the Devil star's last name will appear in the boxes reading from top to bottom.

C _ _ _ □ A R Y

N _ _ W Y _ _ □ K

D □ _ _ R _ _ _ T

W _ _ N _ _ _ □ G

T _ _ R _ _ □ _ O

N _ _ _ H _ _ _ L _ □

BY THE NUMBERS

This wasn't changed in the last round of corrections. Please change it now: Kyle Palmieri and Taylor Hall tied for the team lead in scoring last season. Palmieri had 26 goals and 27 assists, while Hall had 20 goals and 33 assists. So how many points did each of them get?

NICK
LEDDY
#2

NEW YORK ISLANDERS

HOW MUCH CAN A COACHING CHANGE help a struggling club? Just ask the New York Islanders.

As the season began, coach Jack Capuano had the chance to build off of back-to-back 100-point campaigns, two-straight playoff berths and even a trip to the second round, but everything that Capuano had constructed in New York was falling apart. Across the first half of the season, the Islanders' attack was awful, the defense was dire and the goaltending was ghastly, leading to some of the most horrendous hockey the franchise had seen in years. So, when the midpoint of the season passed with the Islanders dead last in

the Eastern Conference, New York canned Capuano and handed the reins to assistant GM and former captain Doug Weight.

The change behind the bench couldn't have worked out any better. New York turned from the fumbling, bumbling club that couldn't do anything right into one of the toughest teams to beat. Weight whipped the Islanders into shape, and they became a high-flying, sharp-shooting, shot-blocking, puck-stopping juggernaut, climbing up the standings with each passing game. The Islanders were so good in the second half of the season that the only team that picked up more points was the league-

best Washington Capitals. Talk about a turnaround!

Right at the center of the Islanders' transformation was captain John Tavares. The high-scoring center rediscovered his magic touch once Weight took over, performing on-ice wizardry and slicing and dicing through defensemen. After a so-so start to his season, Tavares averaged almost a point per game in the second half as New York marched toward a playoff spot.

Tavares could only pull so many rabbits out of his hat, though, and the coaching change came a little too late, as the Islanders finished one point out of the post-season.

LEADERS

POINTS
JOHN TAVARES
66 →

GOALS
ANDERS LEE
34

ASSISTS
JOSH BAILEY
43

PENALTY MINUTES
TRAVIS HAMONIC
60

ICE TIME
NICK LEDDY
22:43

GOALS-AGAINST AVERAGE
THOMAS GREISS
2.69

SAVE PERCENTAGE
JAROSLAV HALAK
.915

PRESIDENT GARTH SNOW
GENERAL MANAGER GARTH SNOW
COACH DOUG WEIGHT
MASCOT SPARKY THE DRAGON

RECORD
41-29-12

HOME
22-12-7

AWAY
19-17-5

POINTS
94

GOALS FOR
239

GOALS AGAINST
238

AVERAGE AGE
28.4

ROOKIES
3

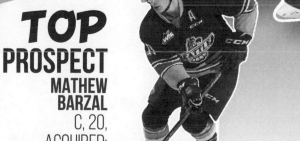

TOP
PROSPECT
MATHEW BARZAL
C, 20,
ACQUIRED:
2015 DRAFT,
16TH OVERALL

HOME JERSEY

DRAW YOUR OWN MASK

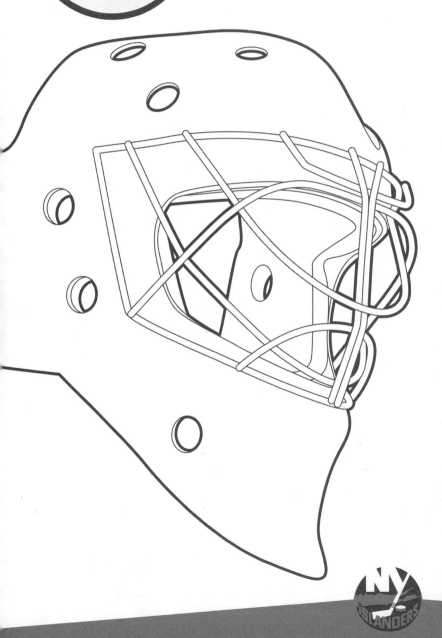

QUIZ

HERE ARE NINE QUESTIONS TO SEE HOW MUCH YOU KNOW ABOUT NEW YORK'S OTHER TEAM, THE ISLANDERS. GET SIX OR MORE RIGHT AND YOU'RE A STARTER. GET THREE OR LESS AND IT'S BACK TO THE MINORS!

1 There is talk that the Islanders may return to their old arena on Long Island. What's it called?

2 New York once won how many Cups in a row?

3 The Isles let coach Jack Capuano go midway through 2016-17. Who did they name as their new coach?

4 GM Garth Snow also played for the Islanders for several seasons. What was his position?

5 A German was between the pipes for the Isles for much of last season? Who is he?

6 New York is captained by John Tavares, who's been with the team since 2009. He was drafted first, second or third overall?

7 Tavares was a special player even as a youngster, granted "exceptional status" so he could play in the Ontario Hockey League at what age?

8 Another German was the team's plus-minus leader last season, finishing a solid plus-25. Who is he?

9 This Islander, with initials CC, was a teammate of Tavares in junior, both playing several seasons with Oshawa. Who is he?

WORD SEARCH

```
Z T K A U B N E P U T S Z
A N E S E R A V A T S J G
S T E N A M C B L I B X A
E N E L L O O L E N I E R
I C L U T T E R B U C K T
D A S A O W G S T Q E A H
E Y R D D A R H E S A K S
N E E K O D A N H I R R N
B I D L B L A A C S E L O
E U N A I A L L R T M P W
R B A A H A K T H G I E W
G I W E K U B O Y C H U K
H T D R E I W E D N C L P
```

TAVARES
WEIGHT
GARTH SNOW
HALAK
LADD
CLUTTERBUCK
BOYCHUK
ANDERS LEE
BAILEY
SEIDENBERG
GREISS
STROME
DE HAAN
CHIMERA

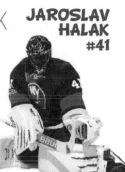

JAROSLAV HALAK #41

FILL IN THE BLANKS

Hidden here is the last name of a current Islander star. Find out who he is by filling in the blank spaces to get the homes of seven NHL teams, either the city or state they play in. We've given you the first and last letters of each city or state and one or two more to get you started. Once you've got them all, the Islander star's name will appear in the boxes reading from top to bottom.

M _ _ _ _ □R _ _ _ _ L

B _ _ _ _ F □_ _ O

N _ S _ _ □_ _ _ _ LE

O _ _ _ _ □_ _ A

A □_ _ Z _ _ _ _ A

M _ _ N _ _ □S _ _ _ A

B _ _ □T _ N

PUZZLE & QUIZ SOLUTIONS ON PAGE 197

BY THE NUMBERS

Brent Sutter was an Islander for more than a decade, playing 694 games with the Isles. He also toiled for Chicago, racking up 417 more games with the Hawks. So how many games total did he play?

MIKA
ZIBANEJAD
#93

NEW YORK
RANGERS

THREE EASTERN CONFERENCE FINAL appearances in five seasons had Broadway buzzing about the potential for a big breakthrough for their beloved Blueshirts, and the rapid fire Rangers came out of the gate flying high with an almost unstoppable offense that started off the season shining brighter than Times Square.

The attack was highlighted by an unexpected star in the early going, as the speed of off-season signing Michael Grabner led the way. It took only 16 games for the Austrian speedster to find the back of the net 10 times, but he was only a small part of New York's

nonstop assault. Five other Rangers caught fire early on, including Mats Zuccarello, Rick Nash and rookie Jimmy Vesey, and by the time the first month of the season was up, the Rangers had the league's most powerful offense. The Rangers' all-out attack continued throughout the campaign, and when the season came to a close, only three teams lit the lamp more often.

And blasting away was what kept New York alive in a division that was tighter than a T-shirt two sizes too small. The Rangers' slow and aging defense started to break down as the season went on, and goaltender Henrik

Lundqvist, known to many as 'King Henrik,' looked more like a joker for the first time in his career. After years of dominating shooters, Lundqvist was only average, finishing the season with the worst statistics of his career and being forced to share the crease with Antti Raanta.

The outstanding offense kept the Rangers in the running, though, as New York finished with a seventh-straight trip to the playoffs. The Blueshirts bowed out in the second round to the Ottawa Senators, but hope remains that the sport's biggest prize will come back to the Big Apple soon.

NEW YORK RANGERS

LEADERS

GOALS
CHRIS KREIDER
28

ASSISTS
MATS ZUCCARELLO
44

PENALTY MINUTES
CHRIS KREIDER
58

ICE TIME
RYAN MCDONAGH
24:21

GOALS-AGAINST AVERAGE
ANTTI RAANTA
2.26

SAVE PERCENTAGE
ANTTI RAANTA
.922

POINTS
MATS ZUCCARELLO
59

PRESIDENT GLEN SATHER
GENERAL MANAGER JEFF GORTON
COACH ALAIN VIGNEAULT

RECORD
48-28-6

HOME
21-16-4

AWAY
27-12-2

POINTS
102

GOALS FOR
253

GOALS AGAINST
216

AVERAGE AGE
28.3

ROOKIES
3

TOP
PROSPECT
LIAS ANDERSSON
C, 19,
ACQUIRED:
2017 DRAFT,
7TH OVERALL

HOME JERSEY

NEW YORK RANGERS

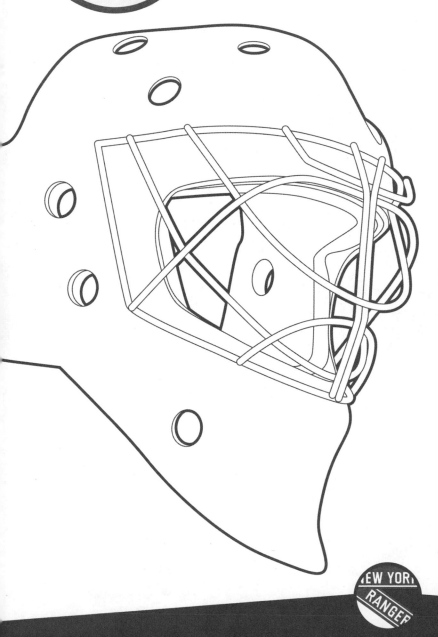

DRAW YOUR OWN MASK

QUIZ

HERE ARE NINE QUESTIONS TO SEE HOW MUCH YOU KNOW ABOUT THE NEW YORK RANGERS. GET SIX OR MORE RIGHT AND YOU'RE A STARTER. GET THREE OR LESS AND IT'S BACK TO THE MINORS!

1 Alain Vigneault is coach of the Rangers, but he previously steered two Canadian teams. Can you name them both?

2 Mats Zuccarello is Norwegian, hailing from which city (hint: it begins and ends with an O)?

3 Goalie Henrik Lundqvist calls Sweden home. His birthplace has just three letters and means "be" in English. Where is it?

4 New York's other goalie has an unusual last name, with three As in just six letters. His first name also begins with an A. Who is he?

5 The Rangers haven't won a Cup since 1994, when their captain wore No. 11. Who was that?

6 This guy was captain, coach and general manager of the Rangers, but he had his number retired by the Bruins. Who was he?

7 New York had four alternate captains last season. Can you name them all?

8 An Austrian led the Rangers with a plus-22 last season. Who was that?

9 Finally, what do the J and T in J.T. Miller stand for?

NEW YORK RANGERS

WORD SEARCH

```
N  H  G  A  N  O  D  C  M  N  S  N  Z
R  W  L  U  N  D  Q  V  I  S  T  J  E
S  I  F  R  O  R  C  G  N  U  E  J  S
N  D  C  I  D  E  S  R  J  G  P  T  V
T  E  T  K  S  N  E  N  S  K  A  M  R
H  F  L  X  N  B  R  W  O  A  N  I  E
E  Z  U  C  C  A  R  E  L  L  O  L  D
G  J  A  L  S  R  S  S  T  S  W  L  I
A  R  E  O  I  G  E  H  Y  S  I  E  E
R  S  N  A  E  Y  T  E  M  D  J  R  R
D  B  G  V  A  H  N  E  R  K  S  L  K
E  E  I  H  A  S  E  O  S  H  O  V  Y
N  U  V  D  G  I  R  A  R  D  I  B  M
```

VIGNEAULT
MCDONAGH
GIRARDI
RICK NASH
STAAL
STEPAN
THE GARDEN
KREIDER
ZUCCARELLO
GRABNER
LUNDQVIST
J.T. MILLER
HAYES
SKJEI

HENRIK
LUNDQVIST
#30

FILL IN THE BLANKS

Hidden here is the last name of a current Ranger star. Find out who he is by filling in the blank spaces to get the nicknames of seven NHL teams. We've given you the first and last letters of each team and one or two more to get you started. The first is the FLAMES. You do the rest. Once you've got them all, the Ranger star's name will appear in the boxes reading from top to bottom.

R _ _ D W _ _ _ _ ☐ S

S _ _ A ☐ S

C _ P _ _ _ ☐ _ _ S

S _ _ ☐ R _ _ S

K _ _ ☐ _ _ S

F _ _ Y ☐ _ _ S

S _ _ _ A _ _ O ☐ S

PUZZLE & QUIZ SOLUTIONS ON PAGE 197

BY THE NUMBERS

The Rangers won an impressive 48 games in 2016-17, but they were better on the road than at home, winning 27 of their 41 away games. How many did they win at home?

KYLE
TURRIS
#7

OTTAWA
SENATORS

IS THERE ANYTHING ERIK KARLSSON CAN'T DO?

The Senators captain stunned everyone in 2015-16 by becoming the first defenseman since the legendary Bobby Orr to lead the league in assists, but the two-time Norris Trophy winner needed to improve his play in his own zone to become the league's top defender once again. So, that's exactly what he did.

In a season in which he skated monster minutes, Karlsson's bombs from the blueline and puck-moving perfection led him to another awesome offensive performance, but he was determined to prove he could be a defensive dynamo, too. Combing style with substance, Karlsson used his world-class skating and incredible on-ice intelligence to transform himself into one of the best two-way defenseman in the league. He wasn't afraid to put his body on the line, either, and when the season ended, he was second in blocked shots, turning aside more rubber than some goaltenders!

Karlsson's brilliance became the cornerstone of a new style of play for the Senators under coach Guy Boucher. With Boucher taking over, opposing teams had to fight for every single inch of ice against the Senators' frustrating defensive shell.

It was easy to cheer for the Senators' success, too, given the difficulties several players and staff faced away from the rink. Before the season began, Bobby Ryan dealt with the loss of his mother, while goaltender Craig Anderson left the team for more than a month to be with his wife, who had been diagnosed with cancer. In the front office, GM Pierre Dorion took over after longtime builder Bryan Murray stepped aside following his own bout with cancer. But no matter what was thrown in their way, Ottawa didn't quit, banding together around their friends and teammates and making it all the way to the Eastern Conference final.

LEADERS

GOALS
KYLE TURRIS
27

ASSISTS
ERIK KARLSSON
54

PENALTY MINUTES
MARK BOROWIECKI
154

ICE TIME
ERIK KARLSSON
26:50

GOALS-AGAINST AVERAGE
CRAIG ANDERSON
2.28

SAVE PERCENTAGE
CRAIG ANDERSON
.926

POINTS
ERIK KARLSSON
71

PRESIDENT TOM ANSELMI
GENERAL MANAGER PIERRE DORION
COACH GUY BOUCHER
MASCOT SPARTACAT

RECORD
44-28-10

HOME
22-11-8

AWAY
22-17-2

POINTS
98

GOALS FOR
206

GOALS AGAINST
210

AVERAGE AGE
28.8

ROOKIES
1

TOP PROSPECT
THOMAS CHABOT
D, 20,
ACQUIRED:
2015 DRAFT,
18TH OVERALL

HOME JERSEY

DRAW YOUR OWN MASK

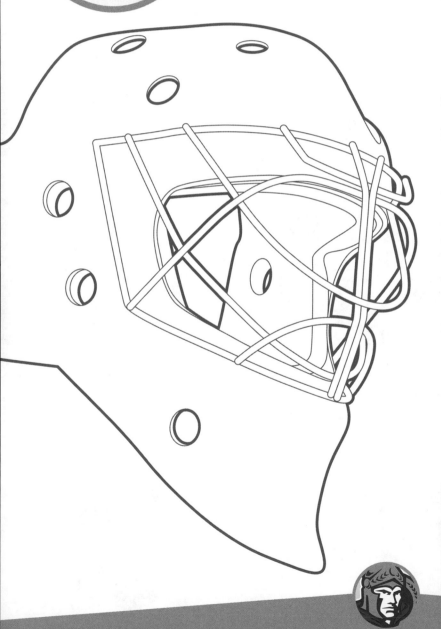

QUIZ

HERE ARE NINE QUESTIONS TO SEE HOW MUCH YOU KNOW ABOUT THE SENATORS. GET SIX OR MORE RIGHT AND YOU'RE A STARTER. GET THREE OR LESS AND IT'S BACK TO THE MINORS!

1 Has a team from Ottawa ever won the Stanley Cup?

2 Guy Boucher also coached the other 1992 expansion team, which is based in Florida. Which team is it?

3 Erik Karlsson succeeded what former Senator as captain in 2014?

4 Karlsson has twice taken home what trophy?

5 Durable Chris Neil was honored by the Senators last December for what accomplishment?

6 What is the name of Ottawa's arena?

7 Kyle Turris' father, Bruce, was so good at his sport that he was named to its Hall of Fame in 2004. What was it (hint: it was once Canada's national game)?

8 Craig Anderson came to Ottawa in a swap for what other goalie?

9 This Senator, whose initials are CC, was born and raised in Ottawa. Who is he?

WORD SEARCH

```
D  N  O  D  N  O  C  K  P  N  A  M  S
B  L  I  E  N  S  I  R  H  C  M  T  I
O  T  U  R  R  I  S  A  A  D  O  T  B
R  A  D  I  E  L  G  L  N  N  R  R  K
O  X  R  T  H  I  Q  A  E  C  V  I  U
W  F  A  N  C  V  D  H  U  H  O  C  P
I  O  S  A  U  N  H  O  F  F  M  A  N
E  J  S  I  O  E  N  T  I  A  G  K  R
C  D  A  D  B  N  O  S  R  E  D  N  A
K  N  R  A  N  E  C  D  A  T  I  N  U
I  O  B  N  K  U  F  U  I  Z  N  E  R
G  T  T  A  Y  P  M  O  T  T  A  T  S
C  H  J  C  L  K  A  R  L  S  S  O  N
```

KARLSSON
CHRIS NEIL
PHANEUF
TURRIS
BOUCHER
BOROWIECKI
CANADIAN TIRE
HOFFMAN
ANDERSON
STONE
BRASSARD
PAGEAU
TOM PYATT
CONDON

CRAIG ANDERSON #41

FILL IN THE BLANKS

Hidden here is the last name of a current Senator star. Find out who he is by filling in the blank spaces to get the nicknames of eight NHL teams. We've given you a bunch of letters for each team to get you started. Once you've got them all, the Senator star's name will appear in the boxes reading from top to bottom.

C _ _ _ U _ _ □ S

P □ N _ _ _ E _ S

F _ _ Y _ _ □ S

A _ _ A □ _ _ N _ _ _ E

I □ _ _ _ _ N _ E _ S

J _ _ T □

C _ _ _ □ T _ S

B _ _ U _ _ □ S

PUZZLE & QUIZ SOLUTIONS ON PAGE 197

BY THE NUMBERS

Mark Borowiecki dished out more hits than any player last season, a whopping 364 in 70 games. That's just over 3, 4, 5 or 6 per game?

CLAUDE GIROUX #28

PHILADELPHIA FLYERS

AS PART OF THEIR 50TH ANNIVERSARY celebration, the Philadelphia Flyers honored late owner Ed Snider, looked back at the brilliance of the Broad Street Bullies and relived the franchise's back-to-back Stanley Cups in 1974 and 1975. The Flyers also celebrated by making some history, though it's not the kind Philadelphia will look back on fondly.

In what was an incredibly frustrating season in the City of Brotherly Love, the Flyers became the first team in NHL history to win 10-straight games yet fail to make the playoffs. It didn't help that Philadelphia's winning ways were followed by several extended losing streaks, including a five-gamer that had

coach Dave Hakstol searching high and low for answers to his team's troubles. The most obvious issue facing the falling Flyers was a goaltending situation that had bigger cracks in it than the Liberty Bell.

Steve Mason had more problems than a math class and that led to the goals against adding up. After two straight years of fantastic play, Mason struggled mightily, posting the worst numbers of his Flyers career. Backup Michal Neuvirth wasn't much better, though. In fact, no goaltender who played at least 20 games had a worse save percentage than Neuvirth!

It didn't help that the Flyers also dealt with disappointing seasons from several play-

ers, including captain Claude Giroux, who scored just 14 goals. Meanwhile, defenseman Shayne Gostisbehere was more Ghost than Bear in his second NHL season. Expected to have a big impact, he failed to match his rookie point total and was even benched a few times.

Luckily for Flyers fans, there was some light at the end of the tunnel. No team made a bigger jump in the draft lottery, as Philadelphia moved from the 13th pick to second overall. This allowed the team to draft Nolan Patrick, giving Philly fanatics something to cheer for at the end of Year 50.

LEADERS

POINTS
JAKUB VORACEK
61

GOALS
WAYNE SIMMONDS
31

ASSISTS
CLAUDE GIROUX
44

PENALTY MINUTES
WAYNE SIMMONDS
122

ICE TIME
IVAN PROVOROV
21:58

GOALS-AGAINST AVERAGE
STEVE MASON
2.66

SAVE PERCENTAGE
STEVE MASON
.908

PRESIDENT PAUL HOLMGREN
GENERAL MANAGER RON HEXTALL
COACH DAVE HAKSTOL

RECORD
39-33-10

HOME
25-11-5

AWAY
14-22-5

POINTS
88

GOALS FOR
212

GOALS AGAINST
231

AVERAGE AGE
27.6

ROOKIES
3

TOP
PROSPECT
NOLAN PATRICK
C, 19,
ACQUIRED:
2017 DRAFT,
2ND OVERALL

HOME JERSEY

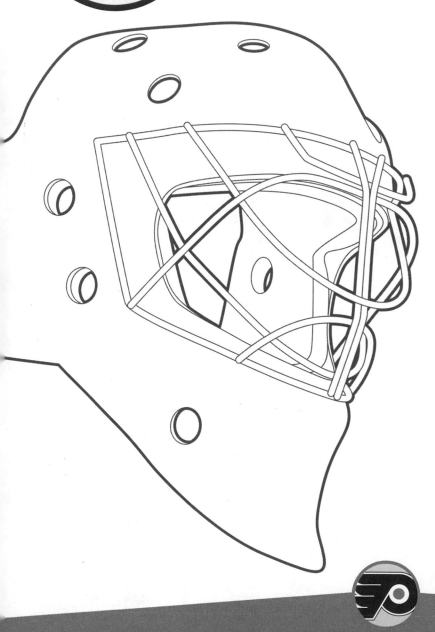

DRAW YOUR OWN MASK

QUIZ

HERE ARE NINE QUESTIONS TO SEE HOW MUCH YOU KNOW ABOUT THE FLYERS. GET SIX OR MORE RIGHT AND YOU'RE A STARTER. GET THREE OR LESS AND IT'S BACK TO THE MINORS!

1 Who's 'Wayne Train'?

2 Flyers coach Dave Hakstol previously led the University of North Dakota to a bunch of Frozen Fours. What is the Frozen Four?

3 Claude Giroux has represented Canada four times in international play and has won two, three or four gold medals?

4 Jakub Voracek shares the NHL record for most points in a single All-Star Game with six. Who is the other player?

5 Which Flyer captured the Calder Trophy as top rookie while with Columbus in 2009?

6 He's nicknamed 'Ghost Bear' and a look at his last name explains why. Who is he?

7 Brayden Schenn's older brother played with Arizona last season. What's his name?

8 The Flyers award a trophy to their MVP each season. What Philadelphia great, remembered for his toothless grin, is it named after?

9 Philly's arena has been known by several names. What does it go by now?

WORD SEARCH

```
Q Z P W B E L L E M A R E
S C H E N N L Y A T R R I
J L I L E H O H Y N E N V
P F C L L A T X E H N O R
R F O S E K I A H S R S G
U A U F O S D B E A I A L
G R T A P T E N C M C M K
O I U R I O N E M E O E K
R U R G T L K O S P U V H
D R I O U L N P C O S E C
M P E D U D F D I L I T S
C A R M S X A E R I N S I
A E R E H E B S I T S O G
```

SCHENN
SIMMONDS
HAKSTOL
WELLS FARGO
GIROUX
VORACEK
COUTURIER
STEVE MASON
RON HEXTALL
BELLEMARE
RAFFL
GUDAS
GOSTISBEHERE
COUSINS

MICHAL NEUVIRTH #30

FILL IN THE BLANKS

Hidden here is the first name of a current Flyer star. Find out who he is by filling in the blank spaces to get the homes of eight NHL teams, either the city or state they play in. We've given you the first and last letters of each city or state and one or two more to get you started. Once you've got them all, the Flyer star's name will appear in the boxes reading from top to bottom.

S _ _ _ J _ _ □ E
C _ _ _ O _ _ □ _ _ A
C _ _ _ _ U □ _ _ _ S
□ _ _ N _ _ E _ _ _ _ _ A
B _ _ S _ _ □ N
V _ _ □ C _ _ _ _ _ _ R
F _ _ O _ _ _ □ A
N _ W _ _ _ _ □ _ Y

PUZZLE & QUIZ SOLUTIONS ON PAGE 197

BY THE NUMBERS

Ex-Flyer Brayden Schenn was one of three players to score 17 power play goals in 2016-17 to top the league. But that left him far short of former Flyer Tim Kerr, who got twice that number back in 1985-86 to set the record. So, how many did Kerr get?

EVGENI
MALKIN
#71

PITTSBURGH
PENGUINS

THE ONLY THING HARDER THAN WINNING THE Stanley Cup is defending the crown. Just don't tell that to the Pittsburgh Penguins.

The year after winning it all, teams tend to suffer from the dreaded Stanley Cup hangover as a result of a short off-season and a summer of celebration. That wasn't the case for Pittsburgh. Instead of slowing down, the Penguins sped up, racing out to 10 victories in their first 15 games and posting the fourth 50-win season in franchise history to finish with 111 points, the second-highest total in franchise history!

It's not hard to understand why, though. Instead of losing players from their cham-pionship team, the Penguins were able to keep most of the Stanley Cup-winning squad together and, another year older and wiser, Pittsburgh ate up the opposition thanks to an all-star attack. No team in the league scored more often than Pittsburgh, who fired home 278 goals, and it was 'Sid the Kid' who led the way. Only months after winning the Conn Smythe Trophy as playoff MVP, Crosby kicked off the new season in style. He had an incredible 17 goals in his first 20 games and finished with 44 to win his second Rocket Richard Trophy.

Right alongside Crosby were Evgeni Malkin and Phil Kessel, who also blasted their way to top-20 point totals. There wasn't another team in the league that had three players combine for as many points.

But just as important as Crosby and Co. in the chase for consecutive Cups was rookie goaltender Matt Murray. One of the team's playoff heroes in 2016, Murray had his first full year in the big league, and he was brilliant, turning in a 32-win season and taking the starting job from veteran Marc-Andre Fleury. With the offense, defense and goaltending clicking as the campaign closed, the Penguins packed their bags for the playoffs and went on to clinch their second-straight Stanley Cup.

LEADERS

POINTS
SIDNEY CROSBY
89

GOALS
SIDNEY CROSBY
44

ASSISTS
PHIL KESSEL
47

PENALTY MINUTES
EVGENI MALKIN
77

ICE TIME
KRIS LETANG
25:31

GOALS-AGAINST AVERAGE
MATT MURRAY
2.41

SAVE PERCENTAGE
MATT MURRAY
.923

PRESIDENT DAVID MOREHOUSE
GENERAL MANAGER JIM RUTHERFORD
COACH MIKE SULLIVAN
MASCOT ICEBURGH

RECORD
50-21-11

HOME
31-6-4

AWAY
19-15-7

POINTS
111

GOALS FOR
278

GOALS AGAINST
229

AVERAGE AGE
28.7

ROOKIES
2

TOP
PROSPECT
DANIEL SPRONG
RW, 20,
ACQUIRED:
2015 DRAFT,
46TH OVERALL

HOME JERSEY

DRAW YOUR OWN MASK

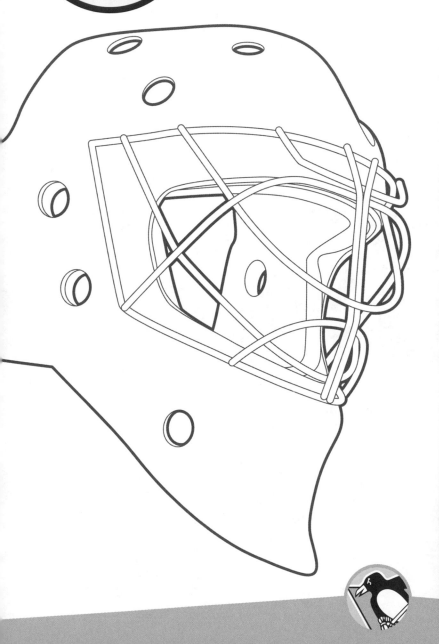

QUIZ

HERE ARE NINE QUESTIONS TO SEE HOW MUCH YOU KNOW ABOUT THE PENGUINS. GET SIX OR MORE RIGHT AND YOU'RE A STARTER. GET THREE OR LESS AND IT'S BACK TO THE MINORS!

1 Sidney Crosby hails from where in Nova Scotia?

2 What did he occasionally hit while practising shooting as a kid?

3 What legendary Penguin did 'Sid the Kid' succeed as captain in Pittsburgh?

4 Evgeni Malkin took home what trophy after the Penguins hoisted the Stanley Cup in 2009?

5 Matt Cullen got some great training as a youth, because his father, Terry, was what?

6 Phil Kessel's sister is a gifted hockey player, too, and has represented the U.S. at many major events, including the last Olympics. What's her name?

7 Chris Kunitz played in two other NHL cities before coming to Pittsburgh. One no longer has a team, though. What cities were they?

8 Matt Murray shared goaltending duties with 'Flower' last season. Who is he?

9 What Penguin regular was drafted 230th and last overall in 2005?

WORD SEARCH

```
S  D  F  Y  A  R  R  U  M  T  T  A  M
T  H  L  N  T  O  L  I  E  K  M  R  C
A  D  E  N  A  V  I  L  L  U  S  U  K
N  L  U  A  S  D  H  J  O  A  I  T  Y
L  P  R  K  R  L  K  B  C  J  W  H  T
E  A  Y  U  O  Y  C  F  N  W  E  E  S
Y  C  Y  N  N  I  K  L  A  M  H  R  I
C  S  E  I  R  N  M  E  I  H  O  F  V
U  I  N  T  B  E  O  Y  S  L  R  O  Q
P  U  X  Z  T  L  U  H  C  S  K  R  N
G  W  O  G  I  L  B  U  I  A  E  D  R
H  I  C  D  M  U  H  N  L  M  O  L  O
S  L  I  M  R  C  R  O  S  B  Y  N  H
```

CROSBY
IAN COLE
KESSEL
KUNITZ
STANLEY CUP
MALKIN
SHEARY
HORNQVIST
CULLEN
SCHULTZ
MATT MURRAY
FLEURY
RUTHERFORD
SULLIVAN

MATT MURRAY #30

FILL IN THE BLANKS

Hidden here is the last name of a current Penguin star. Find out who he is by filling in the blank spaces to get the homes of six NHL teams, either the city or state they play in. We've given you the first and last letters of each city or state and one or two more to get you started. Once you've got them all, the Penguin star's name will appear in the boxes reading from top to bottom.

C _ _ _ U □ _ _ S

B □ _ _ F _ _ _ O

D _ _ T □ _ _ _ T

M _ _ N _ _ □E _ L

C _ _ I _ □ _ O

N _ _ W _ □ _ _ _ K

PUZZLE & QUIZ SOLUTIONS ON PAGE 197

BY THE NUMBERS

Sidney Crosby led the NHL with 44 goals in 2016-17. You could call him 'Mr. Consistency,' as he scored the same number of goals at home and on the road. What number is that?

JOE THORNTON #19

SAN JOSE SHARKS

BEARDED BRILLIANCE IS WHAT THE SHARKS are all about, and it was the bushy-faced Brent Burns who led San Jose into battle in 2016-17.

In previous years, Burns had been a stand-out defender, a smooth-skating, point-pro-ducing weapon on the blueline for the Sharks. But the wild-haired wonder went from good to great in 2016-17and took his game to an all new level. After blowing out his previous career high by putting up 27 goals and 75 points in 2015-16, Burns blasted his way to a new personal best.

With whiskers flying every which way, Burns burned up the ice and scorched the scoresheet with 76 points. The best part of his season, though, was his 29 goals. He became only the ninth different defenseman in NHL history to score that many goals and only the second in the past 20 years!

Burns wasn't the only heavily whiskered hero on the Sharks, however. 'Jumbo' Joe Thornton was once again one of the best offensive forces in San Jose. Thornton, long known as a master passer, finessed his way to another stellar season. It was an impressive feat for the greybeard who remains an elite playmaker into his late 30s.

Joining Thornton as a member of the old guard was longtime Shark Patrick Marleau, and the still-speedy left winger was among the team's best goal scorers, while Joel Ward and Paul Martin, both in their mid-30s, chipped in where they could as part of the oldest roster in the entire league.

But San Jose used their veteran savvy to their advantage. After earning a Stanley Cup final berth as the Western Conference champions last season, the Sharks battled their way right back into the post-season, proving once again that age is just a number, just like their bristly beards are just hair.

Marleau left for Toronto in the off-season, but Burns and Thornton remain to lead the Sharks back into Cup contention in 2017-18.

LEADERS

POINTS
BRENT BURNS
76

GOALS
BRENT BURNS
29

ASSISTS
BRENT BURNS
47

PENALTY MINUTES
MICHEAL HALEY
128

ICE TIME
BRENT BURNS
24:51

GOALS-AGAINST AVERAGE
AARON DELL
2.00

SAVE PERCENTAGE
AARON DELL
.931

GENERAL MANAGER DOUG WILSON
COACH PETER DEBOER
MASCOT SJ SHARKIE

RECORD
46-29-7

HOME
26-11-4

AWAY
20-18-3

POINTS
99

GOALS FOR
219

GOALS AGAINST
200

AVERAGE AGE
29.6

ROOKIES
2

TOP
PROSPECT
JOSH NORRIS
C, 18,
ACQUIRED:
2017 DRAFT,
19TH OVERALL

HOME JERSEY

DRAW
YOUR OWN
MASK

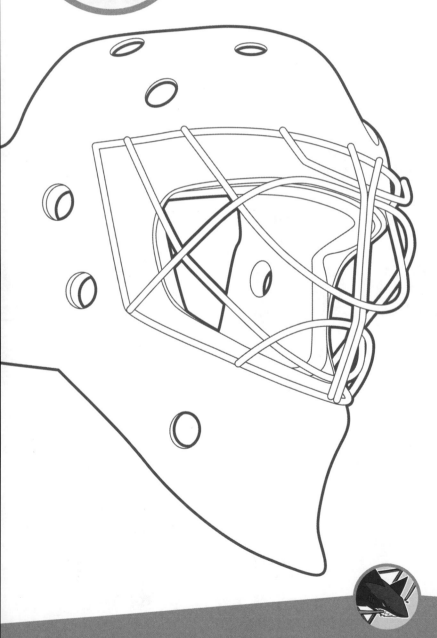

QUIZ

HERE ARE NINE QUESTIONS TO SEE HOW MUCH YOU KNOW ABOUT THE SHARKS. GET SIX OR MORE RIGHT AND YOU'RE A STARTER. GET THREE OR LESS AND IT'S BACK TO THE MINORS!

1 What's the nickname of San Jose's arena?

2 Which Shark captained the U.S. at the World Cup of Hockey (hint: he's also San Jose's captain)?

3 Logan Couture also excelled at what sport as a youngster, winning competitions run by the Blue Jays?

4 Who's 'Jumbo Joe'?

5 What was unique about Joe Thornton winning the Hart Trophy as MVP in 2006?

6 Brent Burns is an animal lover, and his home was appropriately known as what?

7 Thornton was drafted first overall in 1997. What former teammate went right after him?

8 The answer to that question got his 300th, 400th or 500th goal this past February, all of them with San Jose?

9 Martin Jones won a Stanley Cup with which Pacific Division team?

WORD SEARCH

```
P O V I Q N B M R N C P N
L D R A W L E O J R I A P
B R E N T B U R N S S B A
P A R B S L R S H S A R V
G W U R O I S A O C L O E
O N T A O E L P U H V C L
M O U E P E R C H N M E S
A S O A Y N N E J A I K K
X S C U N O T N R O H T I
U L E T M A R T I N N N U
E R S O K U F E I Z N E R
S A T U A E L R A M A T S
C K J T L M H R D E O N U
```

SAP CENTER
DEBOER
PAVELSKI
THORNTON
COUTURE
BRENT BURNS
HALEY
JONES
MARLEAU
JOEL WARD
MARTIN
KARLSSON
VLASIC
BRAUN

MARTIN JONES #31

FILL IN THE BLANKS

Hidden here is the last name of a current Shark star. Find out who he is by filling in the blank spaces to get the nicknames of eight NHL teams. We've given you the first and last letters of each team and one or two more to get you started. Once you've got them all, the Shark star's name will appear in the boxes reading from top to bottom.

C _ P _ ☐ _ _ _ S
A _ _ _ _ _ AN _ ☐E
C _ Y ☐ _ _ _ S
B ☐ U _ _ _ S
K _ _ ☐ _ S
L _ _ _ _ _ ☐N _ NG
G ☐ _ D _ N K _ _ _ G _ _ _ S
R _ _ ☐G _ _ _ S

PUZZLE & QUIZ ANSWERS ON PAGE 197

BY THE NUMBERS

Brent Burns led all players with 320 shots on goal in 2016 -17. He played all 82 games, meaning he averaged nearly 3, 4 or 5 shots per game?

ALEXANDER
STEEN
#20

ST. LOUIS
BLUES

THE 2016-17 SEASON WAS THE TALE OF TWO goaltenders for the St. Louis Blues. But it just so happens both those goaltenders were Jake Allen.

After years splitting time in the St. Louis crease, Allen was given the reins as the Blues' starting goalie when the season began, and the franchise's hopes of taking another step forward after advancing to the Western Conference final the year prior were resting on his heavily padded shoulders. Early in the season, however, 'Jake the Snake' looked like he had been bitten, flopping around his crease and watching softball shots tickle twine far too

often. You would have needed a search party to find Allen on the list of goaltending leaders, and his rough time between the pipes left everyone in St. Louis singing the blues.

But Allen's fortunes changed in February. After falling out of a playoff position, St. Louis fired veteran bench boss Ken Hitchcock and moved Mike Yeo into the top coaching job. The impact on Allen's game was almost immediate. Allen manned the net for 25 of the Blues' final 30 games and there wasn't a single goaltender in the league who was better. After such a bad start, he led nearly

every single goaltending category from February on!

Allen's performance helped the Blues hit all the right notes down the stretch, too. Star scorer Vladimir Tarasenko started flying higher than he had all season, putting pucks in the net with precision and power, while defenseman Alex Pietrangelo looked more like a first-line winger with how often he was stuffing the scoresheet.

It was the best the Blues looked all season, and with no team able to match St. Louis' winning ways, they shot up the standings, earning a playoff spot for the sixth-straight season.

LEADERS

POINTS
VLADIMIR TARASENKO
55

GOALS
VLADIMIR TARASENKO
39

ASSISTS
JADEN SCHWARTZ
36

PENALTY MINUTES
RYAN REAVES
104

ICE TIME
ALEX PIETRANGELO
25:16

GOALS-AGAINST AVERAGE
CARTER HUTTON
2.39

SAVE PERCENTAGE
JAKE ALLEN
.915

PRESIDENT CHRIS ZIMMERMAN
GENERAL MANAGER DOUG ARMSTRONG
COACH MIKE YEO
MASCOT LOUIE

RECORD
46-29-7

HOME
24-12-5

AWAY
22-17-2

POINTS
99

GOALS FOR
233

GOALS AGAINST
216

AVERAGE AGE
28.0

ROOKIES
1

TOP PROSPECT
TAGE THOMPSON
C, 20,
ACQUIRED:
2016 DRAFT,
26TH OVERALL

HOME JERSEY

DRAW
YOUR OWN
MASK

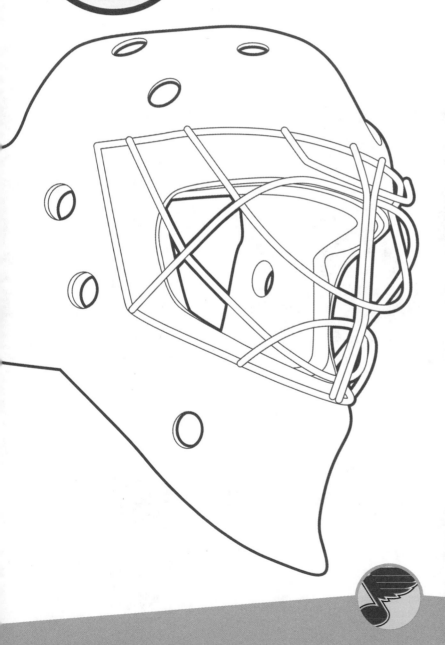

QUIZ

HERE ARE NINE QUESTIONS TO SEE HOW MUCH YOU KNOW ABOUT THE BLUES OF ST. LOO. GET SIX OR MORE RIGHT AND YOU'RE A STARTER. GET THREE OR LESS AND IT'S BACK TO THE MINORS!

1 St. Louis's most famous pair was dubbed 'Hull and Oates' after a musical twosome. What are the players' full names?

2 The Blues were 4-1 winners at the 2017 Winter Classic, held at Busch Stadium. Which team did St. Louis beat?

3 Ken Hitchcock began the year as Blues coach but didn't last. Who's behind the bench now?

4 Alex Pietrangelo has represented Canada five times in international play. How many gold medals has he won?

5 Paul Stastny's dad is a Hall of Famer. What's his name?

6 What sport did hard-hitting Ryan Reaves' father play (hint: he was a Blue Bomber)?

7 St. Louis GM Doug Armstrong has interesting parentage, too. His dad was Neil Armstrong, not the astronaut, but a Hall of Famer. He never played a game, though. What did he do?

8 The Blues have been around for 50 years. They have never won a Cup, but how many times have they played in the final?

9 Jay Bouwmeester was well thought of in the 2002 draft, taken first, second or third overall?

WORD SEARCH

```
P R E T S E E M W U O B N
L C E O L E J A S R M A I
P E R R O N R U D D S T J
O A O K N E S A R A T R A
K E H R K I Y S O D V I K
Y D O A O N E E N H O L E
A A R D T V O U K M M L A
R R B S A N L T I I I A L
A T A E T G I S S L M H L
P T R T R E C D T T I S E
S O L E G N A R T E I P N
S C B N E Q S E L P E U S
C S C H W A R T Z S O N Q
```

STASTNY
SCOTTRADE
PIETRANGELO
MIKE YEO
STEEN
TARASENKO
SCHWARTZ
REAVES
JAKE ALLEN
PARAYKO
UPSHALL
BERGLUND
PERRON
BOUWMEESTER

JAKE ALLEN #34

FILL IN THE BLANKS

Hidden here is the name of a current St. Louis star. Find out who he is by filling in the blank spaces below to get the homes of 11 NHL teams, either the city or state they play. We've given you the first and last letters of each city or state and one or two more to get you started. Once you've got them all, the Blue's name will appear in the boxes reading from top to bottom.

P _ _ _ L _ _ _ _ _ _ ☐ H _ _ A
W _ _ N _ ☐ _ _ _ G
A _ _ _ _ H ☐ _ _ M
D _ _ ☐ R _ _ _ T
A ☐ I _ _ _ _ _ A
T _ M _ _ ☐ B _ _ Y
W _ _ _ H _ _ ☐ _ T _ N
C _ _ _ _ _ A ☐ O
M _ _ _ T _ _ ☐ L
C _ _ ☐ G _ _ _ Y
M _ _ _ _ _ E _ _ ☐ TA

PUZZLE & QUIZ SOLUTIONS ON PAGE 198

BY THE NUMBERS

The NHL expanded in 1967, welcoming the Blues and five other teams. That doubled the league's membership, bringing it to how many teams?

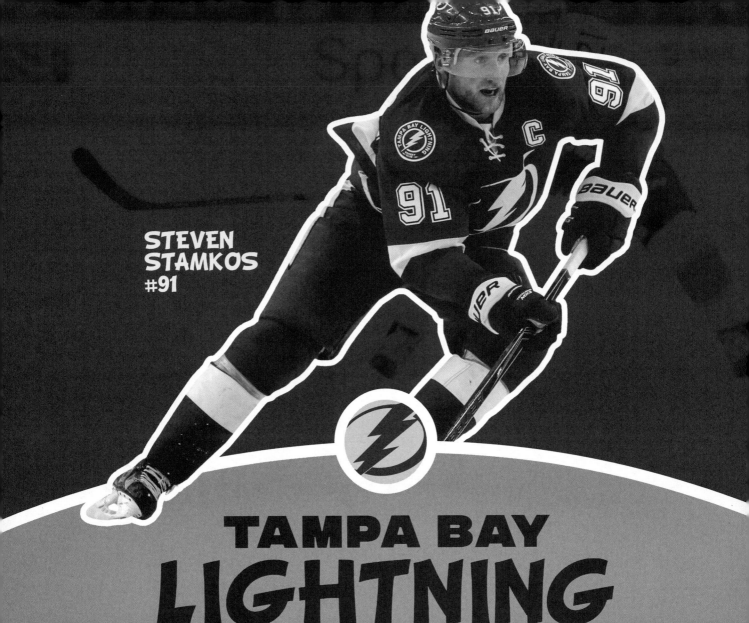

STEVEN
STAMKOS
#91

TAMPA BAY
LIGHTNING

STEVEN STAMKOS HAS HAD SOME BAD BREAKS with injuries over the course of his career, and last season was no different. Just one month into the campaign, the Lightning captain was struck with an injury that derailed what was supposed to be a super season in Tampa Bay.

Making matters worse, Stamkos' injury came just as the Lightning's super sniper seemed to be finding his form. He looked as good as ever, bolting up the ice and unleashing thunderous one-timers that found the back of the net. After Stamkos took an awkward hit in a mid-November game, though, he suffered the knee injury that sidelined him for the remainder of 2016-17.

Stamkos' injury clouded what was supposed to be a bright season in the Sunshine State, but the Lightning weren't about to go out without a fight. When Stamkos went down, up stepped Nikita Kucherov. From mid-November on, Tampa Bay's remarkable Russian winger put the squad on his back. He deked and dangled defensemen before deceiving goaltenders with his electric release, firing his way to 40 goals for the first time in his career.

Kucherov had some help, though, in the form of slippery setup man Jonathan Drouin and two-way talent Ondrej Palat.

Pairing up with Kucherov in attempt to get

Tampa Bay through its tough times was Victor Hedman. The towering defenseman tortured any shooter trying to take him 1-on-1 and made magic with his ability to move the puck up ice. It led Hedman to career highs, as he logged monster minutes and piled points up to the sky.

Yet no matter what Kucherov and Hedman did, the Lightning couldn't fight their way through the storm. Although some had picked Tampa Bay to take the Stanley Cup, the Stamkos-less Lightning missed the playoffs altogether. But after trading Drouin in the off-season, the Bolts are retooling for another run at the Cup in 2017-18.

LEADERS

POINTS
NIKITA KUCHEROV
85

GOALS
NIKITA KUCHEROV
40

ASSISTS
VICTOR HEDMAN
56

PENALTY MINUTES
CEDRIC PAQUETTE
80

ICE TIME
VICTOR HEDMAN
24:30

GOALS-AGAINST AVERAGE
BEN BISHOP
2.55

SAVE PERCENTAGE
ANDREI VASILEVSKIY
.917

PRESIDENT STEVE GRIGGS
GENERAL MANAGER STEVE YZERMAN
COACH JON COOPER
MASCOT THUNDERBUG

RECORD
42-31-10

HOME
23-14-4

AWAY
19-16-6

POINTS
94

GOALS FOR
230

GOALS AGAINST
224

AVERAGE AGE
26.8

ROOKIES
5

HOME JERSEY

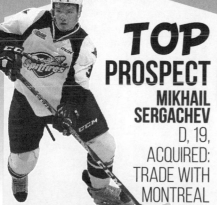

TOP
PROSPECT
MIKHAIL SERGACHEV
D, 19,
ACQUIRED:
TRADE WITH
MONTREAL

DRAW YOUR OWN MASK

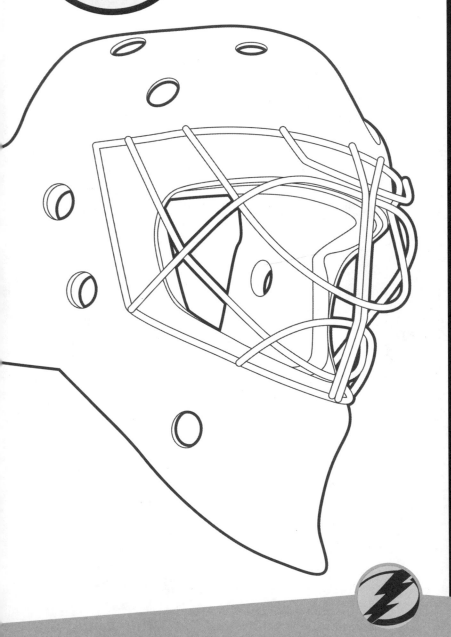

QUIZ

HERE ARE NINE QUESTIONS TO SEE HOW MUCH YOU KNOW ABOUT THE LIGHTNING. GET SIX OR MORE RIGHT AND YOU'RE A STARTER. GET THREE OR LESS AND IT'S BACK TO THE MINORS!

1 'Stevie Y' calls the shots in Tampa. Who is he?

2 Another Steve wears the 'C' in Tampa. Was he drafted first, second or third overall in 2008?

3 Tampa Bay's arena has gone by a number of names over the years. What's it called now?

4 Ryan Callahan previously captained what Metropolitan Division team?

5 The Lightning thought a lot of Victor Hedman, drafting him first, second or fourth overall in 2009?

6 True or false? Spokane-born Tyler Johnson went undrafted.

7 Coach Jon Cooper, who's also a trained lawyer, once aspired to be what kind of agent?

8 Tampa's Vladislav Namestnikov has a name to challenge anyone. In fact, host Jimmy Fallon joked about such hard-to-spell names on what long-running late-night TV show?

9 Why did Tampa Bay choose the nickname Lightning?

WORD SEARCH

```
N A K U C H E R O V S B N
A D N F O T L E R R O H I
M R A R A R T S U S K E J
E O H L S L L A O S M D N
S C A N E R A E I L A M A
T P L G L T D T N H T A M
N N L R N D N O H V S N R
I R A K R I R L L A R F E
K C C J O N C O O P E R Z
O V A P L N E N U F M I Y
V W S M L K F F O I N S R
H L N D I C Q N B E N T S
C U Y I K S V E L I S A V
```

KUCHEROV
STAMKOS
JON COOPER
YZERMAN
PALAT
CALLAHAN
AMALIE ARENA
HEDMAN
VASILEVSKIY
DROUIN
KILLORN
POINT
NAMESTNIKOV
SUSTR

ANDREI VASILEVSKIY #88

FILL IN THE BLANKS

Hidden here is the last name of a current Lightning star. Find out who he is by filling in the blank spaces to get the nicknames of seven NHL teams. We've given you a bunch of letters for each team to get you started. Once you've got them all, the Lightning star's name will appear in the boxes reading from top to bottom.

P _ _ N _ H _ _ _ □
C _ P _ □ _ _ _ S
C _ _ _ □ D _ _ _ _ S
F _ _ A □ _ S
B _ _ _ E J _ C □ _ _ _ S
G □ L _ _ N K _ _ G _ _ _ S
B _ UE □

PUZZLE & QUIZ SOLUTIONS ON PAGE 198

BY THE NUMBERS

Tampa's Victor Hedman was among the league leaders in assists in 2016-17, with 56. He also got 16 goals. So, what percentage of his 72 points were assists (hint: it gives you a number once worn by Phil Esposito, who was the Lightning's first general manager)?

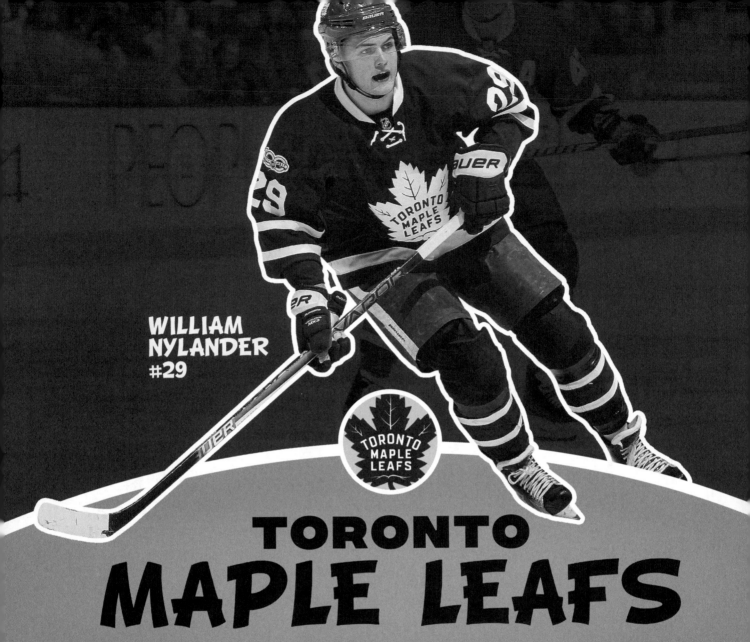

WILLIAM
NYLANDER
#29

TORONTO MAPLE LEAFS

THINGS ARE STARTING TO LOOK UP FOR THE young, Ferrari fast and edge-of-your-pants exciting Maple Leafs, and Toronto has the "Shanaplan" to thank.

The plan is named after Maple Leafs president and former NHLer Brendan Shanahan. To improve a team that was down in the dumps, Toronto traded older players for draft picks that could be used to bring in fresh faces. The Maple Leafs sure accomplished their goal, too. In total, Toronto had an incredible 26 draft picks over the past three years with a dozen in the first three rounds alone. That's a CN Tower-sized collection of prospects!

The Maple Leafs then hit the jackpot when they won the 2016 draft lottery. With the No. 1 pick, they chose Auston Matthews, who wasted no time making NHL history. In his first NHL game, he scored four goals and broke a record that had existed since the NHL's first season in 1917-18. No player had scored four goals in his debut before. By the time the season was over, Matthews was the top scorer on the Leafs and the highest scoring rookie in the entire league.

Matthews wasn't the only youngster who impressed. Nineteen-year-old Mitch Marner, drafted one year earlier, was the team's third-highest scorer, tied with 20-year-old

William Nylander, drafted in 2014. Meanwhile, Morgan Rielly, Nikita Zaitsev and Jake Gardiner, all under 26, were the Maple Leafs' three best defensemen.

With all their up-and-coming youngsters, Toronto had the fifth-youngest team in the league, but coach Mike Babcock led his group of whiz kids through all the ups and downs. And on the second-last day of the season, the Maple Leafs made the playoffs for the first time in four years.

Once mocked as the "Make Believes," the Maple Leafs are no longer the laughing stock of the NHL. Isn't it great when a (Shana)plan comes together?

TORONTO MAPLE LEAFS

LEADERS

POINTS
AUSTON MATTHEWS
69

GOALS
AUSTON MATTHEWS
40

ASSISTS
MITCH MARNER
42

PENALTY MINUTES
MATT MARTIN
123

ICE TIME
MORGAN REILLY
22:10

GOALS-AGAINST AVERAGE
FREDERICK ANDERSON
2.67

SAVE PERCENTAGE
FREDERICK ANDERSON
.918

PRESIDENT BRENDAN SHANAHAN
GENERAL MANAGER LOU LAMORIELLO
COACH MIKE BABCOCK
MASCOT CARLTON THE BEAR

RECORD
40-27-15

HOME
21-13-7

AWAY
19-14-8

POINTS
95

GOALS FOR
251

GOALS AGAINST
242

AVERAGE AGE
26.8

ROOKIES
7

TOP PROSPECT
KASPERI KAPANEN
RW, 21,
ACQUIRED:
TRADE WITH PIT

HOME JERSEY

TORONTO MAPLE LEAFS

DRAW YOUR OWN MASK

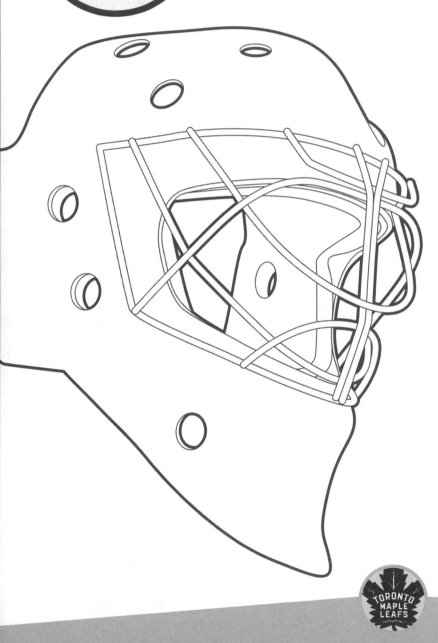

QUIZ

IN HONOR OF A COUPLE OF CELEBRATED LEAFS WHO WORE NO. 9, HERE ARE NINE QUESTIONS ON YOUR FAVORITE TEAM. GET SIX OR MORE RIGHT AND YOU'RE A STARTER. GET THREE OR LESS AND IT'S BACK TO THE MINORS!

1　You probably know that Mike Babcock previously coached Detroit, but do you remember his first NHL team?

2　He had a lot of success with the Red Wings but only won one Cup. True or false?

3　Behind the scenes in Toronto is GM Lou Lamoriello. He also did some coaching in the NHL. Which team did he coach?

4　Brendan Shanahan is now president in Toronto, but he had a long playing career, suiting up for five different teams. He even won three Cups, all of them with which team?

5　The Leafs have had a number of famous captains over the years, but not last season. Instead, they went with four what?

6　Can you name at least three of the four?

7　The Leafs chose first in the 2016 draft and picked Auston Matthews. Had they ever gone first before and, if so, who did they take that time?

8　Matthews was almost eligible for the 2015 draft, but missed the Sept. 17 cutoff date by less than a week. How many days short was he?

9　You probably know that goalie Frederik Andersen was previously with Anaheim, but he was initially drafted by another team in 2010. Which team?

TORONTO MAPLE LEAFS

WORD SEARCH

```
P D K A D R I M C L G O B
N A E N T I L I H K M O C
E D I D Y E P C G T Z A K
F A D E S L H J K A I I Y
L N T R B L K B K S W M D
Z A W S O Y C F Y W E J S
V C Y E P O B U E E H P M
O R E N R A M J L H O A E
R I V X B X O Y M T R Y I
A A X C A M O T E T K Q R
M W O G I B S U I A D E N
O C C D Y M H N L M O G A
K T I P R E D N A L Y N V
```

NYLANDER
AIR CANADA
MATTHEWS
MARTIN
KOMAROV
BABCOCK
VAN RIEMSDYK
ANDERSEN
BOYLE
RIELLY
BOZAK
KADRI
MARNER
SMITH

FREDERIK ANDERSEN #31

FILL IN THE BLANKS

Hidden here is the last name of a current Maple Leaf star. Find out who he is by filling in the blank spaces to get the homes of six NHL teams, either the city or the state in which they play. We've given you the first and last letters of each city or state and one or two more to get you started. Once you've got them all, the Leaf star's name will appear in the boxes reading from top to bottom. Good luck.

E _ _ ☐ O _ _ _ _ N

D ☐ _ L _ S

A ☐ _ _ Z _ _ _ A

V _ _ ☐ _ _ U _ _ R

A _ _ A _ _ ☐ _ M

T _ _ ☐ _ N _ O

PUZZLE & QUIZ SOLUTIONS ON PAGE 198

BY THE NUMBERS

The Maple Leafs have retired a lot of numbers, all the way up to Doug Gilmour's 93. Others include 1, 6, 9, 10, 14 and 27. Add those six up and you get a number that Leaf fans will never forget. What number is that?

DANIEL
SEDIN
#22

VANCOUVER CANUCKS

THEY SAY FIRST IMPRESSIONS ARE EVERYTHING. In hockey, however, they're not the only thing, and the hockey world quickly learned that the quick-start Canucks weren't quite here to stay, because if the 'V' in Vancouver stood for anything in 2016-17, it certainly wasn't victory.

After Vancouver won its first four games to start the season, fans on the West Coast were wide-eyed and willing to believe in their Canucks, but it didn't take long for the doom and gloom to roll in like a storm. Following the four-straight victories, Vancouver lost its next nine games and went on two more streaks of six or more losses in a row. That included a five-game stretch when the Canucks were shutout four times. Fans got used to Vancouver's ugly offense by the end of the season, however. The Canucks finished with the NHL's second-worst attack and were shutout 10 times. On some nights, it looked like Vancouver's shooters couldn't have hit the Pacific Ocean if they were standing right on the coast!

Thankfully, there were a few rays of sunshine peaking through to brighten up the cloud-covered Canucks. As always, the sweet skills of Sedin twins, Daniel and Henrik, were there to liven things up in Vancouver. The dynamic duo remained two of the Canucks' top scorers, using their twin powers to pull off some perfect passing and terrific trickery. But the light that shone the brightest was Bo Horvat, who proved he was all that in his third season in the big league. He set new career bests for goals and points, earning himself a trip the All-Star Game.

All hope was lost in Vancouver by the time April rolled around, though, as the Canucks had sunk to the bottom of the standings, finishing with their fewest points in nearly 20 years.

LEADERS

GOALS
BO HORVAT
20

ASSISTS
HENRIK SEDIN
35

PENALTY MINUTES
NIKITA TRYAMKIN
64

ICE TIME
ALEXANDER ELDER
24:18

GOALS-AGAINST AVERAGE
JACOB MARKSTROM
2.63

SAVE PERCENTAGE
RYAN MILLER
.914

POINTS
BO HORVAT
52

PRESIDENT TREVOR LINDEN
GENERAL MANAGER JIM BENNING
COACH TRAVIS GREEN
MASCOT FIN THE WHALE

RECORD
30-43-9

HOME
18-17-6

AWAY
12-26-3

POINTS
69

GOALS FOR
178

GOALS AGAINST
241

AVERAGE AGE
28.8

ROOKIES
3

TOP
PROSPECT
OLLI **JUOLEVI**
D, 19,
ACQUIRED:
2016 DRAFT,
5TH OVERALL

HOME JERSEY

DRAW YOUR OWN MASK

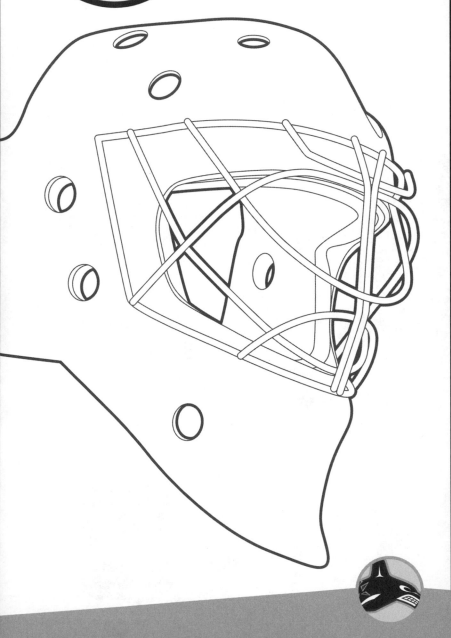

QUIZ

HERE ARE NINE QUESTIONS TO SEE HOW MUCH YOU KNOW ABOUT THE CANUCKS. GET SIX OR MORE RIGHT AND YOU'RE A STARTER. GET THREE OR LESS AND IT'S BACK TO THE MINORS!

1 A disappointing season saw the Canucks fire their coach just a day after it ended. Who was he?

2 Which Sedin twin wears the 'C' in Vancouver? Is it Henrik or Daniel?

3 What trophy have both brothers won?

4 Brandon Sutter is the son of which member of the famous hockey-playing Sutter family?

5 Who did Bo Horvat replace as alternate captain last season?

6 Luca Sbisa was born in Italy but played for what country at the 2010 Olympics in Vancouver?

7 Markus Granlund's older brother plays for the Wild. What's his name?

8 'The Russian Rocket' is one of four Canucks whose numbers have been retired. Who is he?

9 What sickness caused a number of Canucks to miss games in 2016-17?

WORD SEARCH

```
T E G A R E T T U S E N Z
E S N A J R A N R N K J G
L W O N A I I L N I U L R
M O R T S K R A M W R U A
B R T M H S L N T T K C N
E R A C O S E O O N E A L
N U V R E O E H R I A S U
N B R F S N A E V D W B N
I I O M I L L E R E S I D
N S H A E D M K O S N S A
G R O G E R S A R E N A M
Y E B A E R T S C H I J T
N O P T S Q C E B O M K G
```

JACOB MARKSTROM #25

BO HORVAT
SEDIN TWINS
EDLER
BURROWS
SUTTER
TANEV
LUCA SBISA
MILLER
ROGERS ARENA
MARKSTROM
BAERTSCHI
ERIKSSON
GRANLUND
BENNING

FILL IN THE BLANKS

Hidden here is the first initial and last name of a current Canuck star. Find out who he is by filling in the blank spaces to get the homes of six NHL teams, either the city or state they play in. We've given you the first and last letters of each city or state and one or two more to get you started. Once you've got them all, the Canuck star's name will appear in the boxes reading from top to bottom.

F _ _ O _ _ _ ☐ A

P _ _ _ T ☐ B _ _ _ _ H

M _ _ _ T _ _ ☐ _ L

E ☐ _ _ O _ _ _ _ N

A _ _ ☐ Z _ _ _ A

C _ _ _ O _ _ _ ☐ A

PUZZLE & QUIZ SOLUTIONS ON PAGE 198

BY THE NUMBERS

The Sedin twins may look alike, but their numbers aren't quite the same. Daniel has racked up 986 career points, Henrik 1,021. So, Henrik has got how many more than his bro?

MARC-ANDRÉ
FLEURY
#17

VEGAS
GOLDEN KNIGHTS

AFTER A MONTHS-LONG SEARCH FOR THE league's next franchise, it was the Vegas Golden Knights who hit the jackpot as the NHL decided to gamble and become the first professional sports league to put a team in Las Vegas.

While there was no on-ice action in Vegas in 2016-17, there were few teams as exciting to follow away from the rink as Golden Knights assembled their very own round table of brilliant hockey minds. Sitting at the head of the table is GM George McPhee, the longtime architect of the Washington Capitals, who embraced his new challenge head

on. In his first major move as the builder behind the Sin City squad, McPhee went out and snapped up coach Gerard Gallant, the former Florida Panthers bench boss, to lead the Golden Knights into battle.

But McPhee's work was far from over with a coaching hire. The Golden Knights made history when they inked Reid Duke, an undrafted free agent, to become the franchise's first official player, and surprised everyone with a shocking signing only months later. With several teams chasing after free agent Vadim Shipachyov, the Golden Knights anted up, pushed all their chips into the middle

and went all-in on the Russian center, signing him to a two-year deal and snatching him away from the rest of his suitors.

All the off-season work led up to Vegas' own personal roster roulette, however, as the Golden Knights prepared for the expansion draft. McPhee and his staff spent countless hours pouring over every scenario in hopes of building a roster that won't just participate in the 2017-18 season, but actually push for a playoff spot. And with the draft rules stacking the deck in the Golden Knights' favor, there's no reason why the first season in Vegas can't be one to remember.

MATCHUP

PRESIDENT KERRY BUBOLZ
GENERAL MANAGER GEORGE MCPHEE
COACH GERARD GALLANT

The bulk of the Golden Knights roster was acquired at the expansion draft on June 21st. The Knights selected a player from each of the 30 existing teams. A dozen of those players are listed here. Can you match each of them with his former team?

CALVIN PICKARD	DETROIT RED WINGS
CODY EAKIN	BUFFALO SABRES
THOMAS NOSEK	VANCOUVER CANUCKS
LUCA SBISA	PITTSBURGH PENGINS
JAMES NEAL	DALLAS STARS
BRAYDEN MCNABB	NEW YORK RANGERS
WILLIAM CARRIER	NASHVILLE PREDATORS
CLAYTON STONER	EDMONTON OILERS
MARC-ANDRÉ FLEURY	WASHINGTON CAPITALS
NATE SCHMIDT	COLORADO AVALANCHE
GRIFFIN REINHART	ANAHEIM DUCKS
OSCAR LINDBERG	LOS ANGELES KINGS

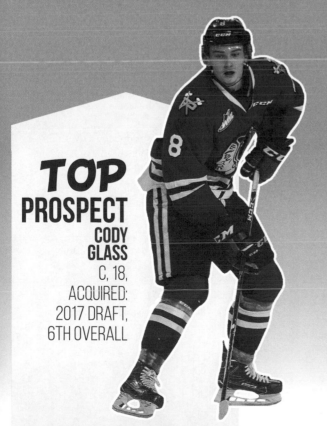

TOP PROSPECT
CODY GLASS
C, 18,
ACQUIRED:
2017 DRAFT,
6TH OVERALL

DRAW YOUR OWN MASK

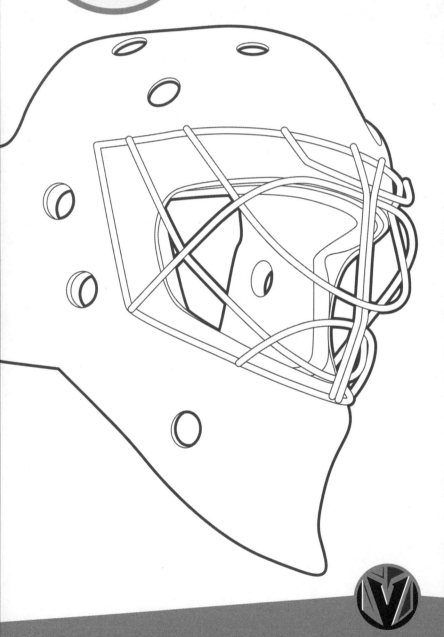

QUIZ

HERE ARE NINE QUESTIONS TO SEE HOW MUCH YOU KNOW ABOUT THE NHL'S NEWEST TEAM. GET SIX OR MORE RIGHT AND YOU'RE A STARTER. GET THREE OR LESS AND IT'S BACK TO THE MINORS!

1 With the coming of the Golden Knights, the NHL now has an odd number of teams. How many?

2 While Vegas got a team, a Canadian city that was also in the running fell short in its bid. What city?

3 What famous Las Vegas casino – also known for its fights – hosted an outdoor NHL exhibition game way back in 1991?

4 Mike Foligno is a scout with the Knights and also the father of two hockey-playing sons. Can you name them both?

5 The music group The Killers officially opened the Knights arena in April of 2016. What is the name of the team's rink?

6 GM George McPhee was previously with the Washington Capitals. Which superstar did he draft first overall in 2004?

7 True or false? Las Vegas once had a team in the Canadian Football League.

8 Las Vegas also hosts what big NHL annual event?

9 The Knights will play in a color that's also popular with the Kings and the Penguins. What color is that?

WORD SEARCH

```
N H G A N O D C G N S N Z
R W S A G E V S A L T N E
S I F R O R C K L U H J S
N D C I D E N R L L Y T V
T T M O B I L E A R E N A
H F L X G B R W N A L I C
E Z U H C A A E T L O I D
G J T L D R S S T E F L I
A S E A D G E H E I L E E
R S V S E Y T H C D L R R
D E G V E X P A N S I O N
N E I H A C P O S H B V Y
N U V D M I R A R D I B M
```

GALLANT
KNIGHTS
T-MOBILE ARENA
BILL FOLEY
NHL AWARDS
EXPANSION
MCPHEE
PACIFIC
NEVADA
LAS VEGAS

FILL IN THE BLANKS

Hidden here is the last name of the Golden Knights' new GM. Find out who he is by filling in the blank spaces below to get the nicknames of six NHL teams. We've given you the first and last letters of each team and one or two more to get you started. Once you've got them all, the GM's name will appear in the boxes reading from top to bottom.

F __ A □ __ S

C __ N __ □ __ S

C __ □ I __ __ __ LS

S □ __ R __ S

D □ V __ __ __ S

I __ L __ N __ □ __ S

PUZZLE & QUIZ SOLUTIONS ON PAGE 199

BY THE NUMBERS

This one is a bit tricky, so good luck with it. The NHL began play 100 years ago with just four teams. Las Vegas is now the league's 31st club. So, the NHL is how much bigger now than it was then?

ALEX OVECHKIN #8

WASHINGTON CAPITALS

ALEX OVECHKIN HAS SCORING TITLES, MVPs and a long list of other awards. He's earned himself the Washington Capitals' captaincy, scored highlight-reel tallies and is undeniably one of the best pure goal scorers the league has ever seen. But the one thing 'The Great 8' doesn't have to his name is a Stanley Cup.

Ovechkin wanted to change that in 2016-17, however, and doing so meant changing his role. So, while he took the ice with the same rocket-like speed, video-game skill and cannon-blast shot that he's always possessed, Ovechkin took on fewer minutes, buying into a smaller role and saving himself for the

playoffs. But the result was what some would call a down year for the superstar sniper, as he failed to reach the 50-goal mark for the first time in the past four years.

Others stepped up, though, and center Nicklas Backstrom rose to the challenge, controlling play with perfect passing and superhuman vision. Backstrom's passes were crisp and clean as he racked up the second-most assists and fourth-most points in the league on a Capitals club that assaulted the opposition net and scored a whopping 261 goals!

As the season moved along, Washington looked harder to get by than security at the

White House, but the Capitals weren't about to stop bulking up for what stood to be a memorable playoff run. At the deadline, Washington went out and made a sumo wrestler's cannonball-sized splash by beating out every other team for the services of defenseman Kevin Shattenkirk. The addition only added another rock to the fortress that was built around standout stopper Braden Holtby.

Washington crushed the competition en route to a second-straight Presidents' Trophy, but the real title the team wanted to win was lost again, as Ovechkin and the Capitals bowed out to archrival Sidney Crosby and the Pittsburgh Penguins in the second round.

capitals

WASHINGTON

LEADERS

GOALS
T.J. OSHIE
33

ASSISTS
NICKLAS BACKSTROM
63

PENALTY MINUTES
TOM WILSON
133

ICE TIME
JOHN CARLSON
22:42

GOALS-AGAINST AVERAGE
PHILIPP GRUBAUER
2.04

SAVE PERCENTAGE
PHILIPP GRUBAUER
.926

POINTS
NICKLAS BACKSTROM
86

PRESIDENT DICK PATRICK
GENERAL MANAGER BRIAN MACLELLAN
COACH BARRY TROTZ
MASCOT SLAPSHOT

RECORD
55-19-8

HOME
32-7-2

AWAY
23-12-6

POINTS
118

GOALS FOR
261

GOALS AGAINST
177

AVERAGE AGE
28.4

ROOKIES
2

HOME JERSEY

TOP PROSPECT

ILYA SAMSONOV
G, 20,
ACQUIRED:
2015 DRAFT,
22ND OVERALL

WASHINGTON
capitals

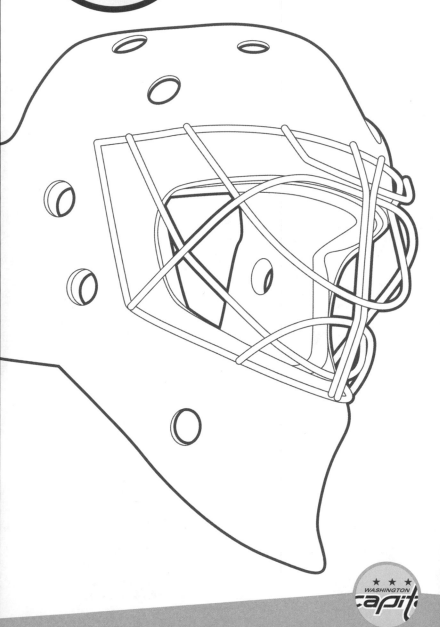

DRAW YOUR OWN MASK

QUIZ

HERE ARE NINE QUESTIONS TO SEE HOW MUCH YOU KNOW ABOUT THE CAPITALS. GET SIX OR MORE RIGHT AND YOU'RE A STARTER. GET THREE OR LESS AND IT'S BACK TO THE MINORS!

1 What team trophy did the Capitals win for the second season in a row in 2016-17?

2 Barry Trotz was previously with the Predators. He coached in Nashville for 12, 13, 14 or 15 years?

3 It's been a while since Alex Ovechkin won the Art Ross Trophy as leading scorer. Was it in 2008, 2010 or 2012?

4 Brooks Orpik was born a few months after the Miracle on Ice. He was named after the coach of that 1980 U.S. Olympic team. Who was that?

5 Which Capital player's first and middle names are Timothy and Jimothy?

6 True or false? Nicklas Backstrom has represented Sweden many times but has never won a gold medal.

7 What other Swedish born Capital is known as both 'MoJo and 'Mackan'?

8 What trophy did former Capital Justin Williams win following the 2014 playoffs?

9 Which Cap has a last name that's also a breed of dog?

WASHINGTON
capitals

WORD SEARCH

```
T  E  G  A  N  I  S  K  A  N  E  N  Z
E  J  N  A  J  A  A  N  R  D  K  J  E
L  O  O  N  A  R  I  L  N  U  K  X  T
G  D  A  S  L  K  N  O  Z  I  R  E  V
A  E  E  M  H  U  L  N  T  N  K  R  W
E  L  A  C  O  I  E  O  O  A  E  A  I
B  D  E  R  E  T  E  H  R  U  A  R  L
A  V  P  F  S  F  A  S  T  I  W  R  L
O  I  Z  O  U  L  P  G  Y  S  I  L  I
K  S  V  A  E  L  L  E  R  D  L  P  A
R  Q  M  A  V  H  K  E  R  A  S  E  M
Y  E  P  N  O  S  S  N  A  H  O  J  S
M  O  R  T  S  K  C  A  B  O  N  L  G
```

OVECHKIN
VERIZON
ORPIK
BACKSTROM
BARRY TROTZ
T.J. OSHIE
ELLER
JOHANSSON
WILLIAMS
WILSON
BEAGLE
NISKANEN
ALZNER
KUZNETSOV

BRADEN HOLTBY #70

FILL IN THE BLANKS

Hidden here is the first name of a current Capital star. Find out who he is by filling in the blank spaces to get the nicknames of five NHL teams. We've given you a bunch of letters for each team to get you started. Once you've got them all, the Cap star's name will appear in the boxes reading from top to bottom.

P __ E __ __ __ T □ __ S

P __ N T __ __ __ __ □ S

C __ □ __ T __ __ __ S

D __ __ __ □ L S

B __ __ __ C K __ __ __ __ __ □ S

PUZZLE & QUIZ SOLUTIONS ON PAGE 198

BY THE NUMBERS

Netminder Braden Holtby was the NHL's best at shutting the door on opponents in 2016-17, racking up nine shutouts in 63 games. On average, that's one per how many games?

PATRIK
LAINE
#29

WINNIPEG
JETS

WITH A ROSTER FULL OF YOUNG TALENT, veteran leadership and a sharpshooting new star, some believed the Winnipeg Jets could fly under the radar, soar up the standings and reach their highest point since their return to Manitoba's capital.

Offensively, that was surely the case. The Jets' young offense was as bright as any in the league. Center Mark Scheifele hitting new personal bests by cracking the 30-goal and 80-point barriers for the first time in his career, second-year speedster Nikolaj Ehlers burned up the ice and lit up the score sheet with his first 20-goal campaign and the always consistent Blake Wheeler brought the veteran savvy as the team's new captain while piecing together a second-straight 70-point year.

The highlight of the season, though, was sharpshooting sniper Patrik Laine. Drafted second overall in 2016 by the Jets, the new 'Finnish Flash' took the league by storm. Every perfect pass was ready for blast off when it came Laine's way, and by the time the season was through, only six skaters in the entire league had turned the red light on more often. And Laine sure knew how to score in bunches, too. No player had more three-goal games than Laine, which earned him the nickname 'Hat Trick Laine.'

But not even the high-powered offense could stop Winnipeg's goaltending from sending the squad into a tailspin. Connor Hellebuyck was given the crease and asked to pilot the Jets to the playoffs, but after a solid rookie season, the sophomore hit a serious slump and backup Michael Hutchinson couldn't pull the parachute to save the Jets' post-season hopes.

Even though the Jets hit some turbulence in 2016-17, the future still looks bright. With a new Finnish superstar-in-the-making to go with their young core and top talent, the Jets look primed and ready to fly into Stanley Cup contention in the near future.

LEADERS

POINTS
MARK SCHEIFELE
82

GOALS
PATRICK LAINE
36
—
ASSISTS
MARK SCHEIFELE
50
—
PENALTY MINUTES
DUSTIN BYFUGLIEN
117
—
ICE TIME
DUSTIN BYFUGLIEN
27:26
—
GOALS-AGAINST AVERAGE
CONNOR HELLEBUYCK
2.89
—
SAVE PERCENTAGE
CONNOR HELLEBUYCK
.907

PRESIDENT JIM LUDLOW
GENERAL MANAGER KEVIN CHEVELDAYOFF
COACH PAUL MAURICE
MASCOT MICK E. MOOSE

RECORD
40-35-7

HOME
22-18-1

AWAY
18-17-6

POINTS
87

GOALS FOR
246

GOALS AGAINST
255

AVERAGE AGE
26.1

ROOKIES
3

TOP
PROSPECT
KYLE CONNOR
LW, 20,
ACQUIRED:
2015 DRAFT,
17TH OVERALL

HOME JERSEY

DRAW YOUR OWN MASK

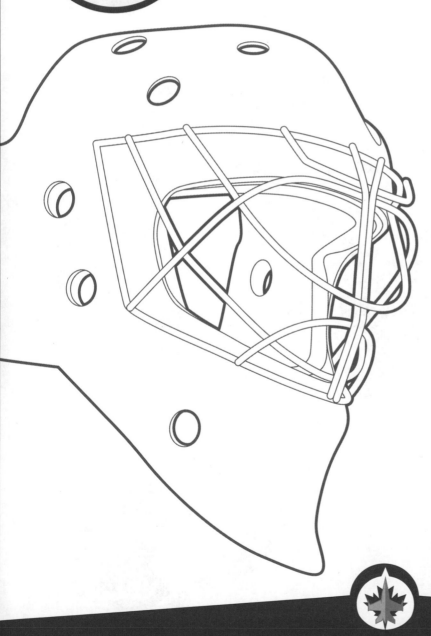

HERE ARE NINE QUESTIONS TO SEE HOW MUCH YOU KNOW ABOUT THE RESURGENT JETS. GET SIX OR MORE RIGHT AND YOU'RE A STARTER. GET THREE OR LESS AND IT'S BACK TO THE MINORS!

1 Dustin Byfuglien is an alternate captain with the Jets. Where else did he wear an 'A'?

2 Who did Blake Wheeler succeed as captain of the Jets?

3 Coach Paul Maurice has been around. One team even fired him twice. Which team was that?

4 Both the Jets and their AHL affiliate play at the MTS Centre. What's the name of their minor league team?

5 Patrik Laine was very well thought at the 2016 draft, going second overall. Who went before him?

6 Who did the Jets choose first in the 2011 draft, which marked their return to the NHL?

7 Adam Lowry's dad, Dave, played with what NHL team (hint: Adam was born in St. Louis)?

8 What Winnipeg regular has the same initials as the letters that appear in the Montreal Canadiens logo?

9 How many goals did Mathieu Perreault score in a 2015 game to equal a team record?

WORD SEARCH

```
T  E  Y  E  S  S  I  R  R  O  M  N  Z
R  S  N  A  J  V  A  N  S  N  K  J  Y
B  S  C  H  E  I  F  E  L  E  K  L  R
O  O  R  T  S  K  H  A  M  W  C  U  W
B  Y  F  U  G  L  I  E  N  T  Y  C  O
W  R  A  C  E  S  C  O  Q  A  U  A  L
H  U  V  R  E  I  A  O  B  L  B  S  M
E  B  S  F  R  M  A  U  P  D  E  B  A
E  I  O  U  T  L  O  E  R  P  L  U  D
L  S  A  S  E  R  M  K  O  A  L  S  A
E  M  O  R  T  S  N  E  I  E  E  A  M
R  P  B  A  E  R  T  N  C  H  H  J  T
N  O  M  T  S  C  E  N  T  R  E  K  G
```

MAURICE
WHEELER
HELLEBUYCK
SCHEIFELE
BYFUGLIEN
LAINE
MTS CENTRE
EHLERS
COPP
TROUBA
ADAM LOWRY
ENSTROM
POSTMA
MORRISSEY

CONNOR HELLEBUYCK #37

FILL IN THE BLANKS

Hidden here is the last name of a current Jet star. Find out who he is by filling in the blank spaces to get the nicknames of five NHL teams. We've given you the first and last letters of each team and one or two more to get you started. Once you've got them all, the Jet star's name will appear in the boxes reading from top to bottom.

F ☐ _ E _ S

A _ ☐ _ _ A _ C _ E

O ☐ L _ _ _ S

B _ _ U _ _ ☐ S

D ☐ _ _ I _ S

PUZZLE & QUIZ SOLUTIONS ON PAGE 198

BY THE NUMBERS

Of the NHL's top 20 scorers in 2016-17, it was the Jets' Mark Scheifele who made the most of his efforts. He scored 32 times on just 160 shots. So, how many shots did he take per goal?

THE SCIENCE OF
HOC

KEY

GO BEHIND THE SCENES AS
HOCKEY'S OFF-ICE EXPERTS TEACH
YOU ALL YOU NEED TO KNOW ABOUT
THE SCIENCE OF THE GAME AND
HOW KIDS CAN TRAIN TO BECOME
FUTURE NHL STARS

HOW DOES A ZAMBONI WORK?

DISCOVER OUT HOW THE ICONIC MACHINE MAGICALLY TURNS ROUGH ICE INTO SMOOTH SKATING

BY MATT CARLSON

Hockey wouldn't be the fast-paced game it is today without the Zamboni. So every hockey player and fan knows how a Zamboni works, right? Maybe not.

Technically, a Zamboni is a "Zamboni ice resurfacer" or "Zamboni ice resurfacing machine." Frank J. Zamboni & Co., which makes the famous machines, has delivered more than 11,000 around the world and keeps improving them.

The first genuine Zamboni – and the first-ever self-propelled ice resurfacing machine – was invented and sold by Frank Zamboni in 1949. The company, based near Los Angeles, Calif., has a colorful history. It also makes machines in Brantford, Ont.

Frank and his brother were experts in the ice and refrigeration business. They opened a rink in the town of Paramount, Calif., in 1940 that's still there today. Back then, resurfacing a rink took three or four workers over an hour to complete. Frank worked for nearly 10 years to develop a Zamboni Model A machine that would do it faster and better.

THEY CAN REACH SPEEDS OF ALMOST 10 MILES PER HOUR

Ice surfaces get torn up from all kinds of skating, not just hockey. Skate blades cut grooves into the ice even when hockey players are striding. When players stop and turn quickly, they dig in even deeper, and create ruts and lots of snow. The Zamboni fixes this.

Some Zambonis have electric motors and are powered by batteries. Others use propane gas, natural gas or gasoline as fuel. These machines have filters so the air in a rink stays clean. They can reach speeds up of almost 10 mph, and just like cars and trucks, they have a steering wheel and a foot pedal. When a Zamboni resurfaces a hockey rink, it travels about 0.75 of a mile, and each time it can remove almost 2,500 pounds of snow and leave behind 1,500 pounds of water.

A car would slip all of over the ice, but a Zamboni doesn't. Why? Each tire on a machine has small metal studs that delicately grab the ice.

All Zamboni machines have the same basic shape, but the resurfacers come in different sizes because some rinks are busier than others. Larger machines cost over $100,000.

HERE'S HOW A ZAMBONI DOES ITS JOB

#1 Most of the work happens at the back of a Zamboni, where a giant, sharp blade extends across the entire width of the machine. As the machine moves forward, the blade shaves the ice and scrapes up snow. The driver can adjust the depth of the shaving.

#2 The snow is collected and moved by large spinning screws called "augers". Rotating brushes on the sides of the machines collect snow that's along the boards of the rinks.

#WCH2016

#3 A "horizontal auger" extends across the back of the machine to gather the snow. The snow is lifted into a snow tank – the big bin on top of the machine – by a "vertical auger" that runs down the middle of the back of the machine.

#4 At the same time, the machine shoots jets of water down from a wash-water tank onto the ice to clean it. The water is quickly collected by a rubber squeegee, a huge version of ones used on car windows at gas stations, then sucked up into a tank by a vacuum.

#5 The Zamboni then spreads a thin coat of clean, warm "ice-making" water from the back of the machine to create a fresh new layer on the ice surface. The ice-making water is then smoothed out by a big towel-like flap at the tail.

#6 Both the cleaning and ice-making water is stored in tanks in the machine. The operator can refill and drain the tanks.

#7 After resurfacing, the driver dumps the snow into a drain or out a door. The big snow tank tips forward to make this easy.

HOW ARE PUCKS MADE?

DISCOVER THE SECRET RECIPE BEHIND BAKING RUBBER BISCUITS

BY MATT CARLSON

Hockey pucks are more than just black rubber discs, and they need to be perfect, especially in the NHL.

Sher-Wood Hockey, the world's leading puck-maker and official puck-provider to the NHL since 1988, takes the job seriously.

All real hockey pucks have the same specs. They measure one inch thick and three inches in diameter, and they weigh six ounces. Sher-Wood, which is based in Sherbrooke, Que., now makes some of its pucks in Slovakia, but the pucks that go to the NHL and other pro teams are made in Canada.

"No matter where our pucks are made, they're designed to perform exactly the same for everybody who uses them," said Sher-Wood's Sean McKenna. "We're not looking to cut corners for certain customers.

"And the performance of our pucks today allows guys like Connor McDavid and Sidney Crosby to perform the way they perform."

Sher-Wood literally cooks up pucks using a secret recipe. The ones shipped to the NHL start in a facility near Montréal and in a room Sher-Wood calls the "kitchen."

RECIPE FOR COOKING
RUBBER COOKIES

#1

The material that goes into a puck is melted into a thick liquid and stirred in an automatic blender. About 65 to 70 percent of the "puck soup" is rubber or synthetic rubber. The rest is made up of fillers and stabilizers. Sher-Wood won't divulge those ingredients that give its finished pucks the best possible properties, including hardness and bounce.

#2

Once the puck soup is thoroughly heated and blended, it goes into an "extrusion" machine. After the material starts to cool and solidify, the machine can press out a long, round rod of gooey puck material that's roughly three inches thick. It's like making giant logs using a Play-Doh press.

#3

The puck material is sliced into pieces, called "slugs," that are about one inch thick. Think of neatly cutting a perfectly round meatloaf.

#4

Each of the slugs is placed into a mold that's the size of an actual puck. The slug is allowed to "cure" in the mold, where oils and other elements are allowed to settle. Excess moisture also "sweats" out of the slug.

#5

When ready, each puck is pressed by a machine in the mold at the right temperature, and to the proper weight and size. The mold forms each puck's textured edge and smooth faces.

#6

The pucks are still hot when they come out of their molds. Any excess material, called "flash" is trimmed away. The pucks are allowed to cool and then packed in boxes.

#7

Pucks heading to the NHL and other elite teams are shipped in the boxes to Sher-Wood's main facility in Sherbrooke. There, multicolored team logos are applied precisely using silk screening machines. NHL teams get 2,500 to 3,000 game pucks per season, plus thousands more for practices.

#8

Pucks are inspected visually and tested to make sure the specs are right. A machine called a "durometer" measures hardness. Sher-Wood also uses other methods, including drop tests, to measure the rebounding and resilience of the pucks.

HOW ARE STICKS MADE?

LEARN WHAT GOES INTO MAKING WEAPONS FOR ON-ICE WARRIORS
BY MATT CARLSON

Technology has changed hockey sticks forever.

For decades, sticks were crafted from wood only. Eventually, many had coatings, often made from fiberglass.

In the 1980s, a company called Easton Sports pioneered two-piece hockey sticks. The shafts were made from aluminum, but the blades were still made from wood and fiberglass, and they were attached using heated glue.

Shafts made from composites – blended materials like a strong, high-tech plastic – first appeared in the 1990s. Composite materials can have different ingredients, but they're generally formed from threads of carbon, fiberglass – sometimes even bulletproof Kevlar – that are heated and pressed together with special glue, called "resin."

Easton's Synergy sticks, introduced in 2001, were the first successful one-piece all-composite sticks. The silver Synergy models were expensive and lacked the natural "puck feel" of wood sticks but allowed players to transfer more energy into faster and quicker shots.

Manufacturers have made big improvements since then. Now one-piece composite models are the norm for all players.

STICK-MAKING
STEP BY STEP

#1 Threads called "filaments" are pressed and rolled together into long sheets on machines. It's like having thousands of tiny pieces of spaghetti, all lined together, go through rollers to create one flat sheet of pasta.

#2
The sheets are about four feet wide and have a thin plastic coating on each side to keep them moist with the glue-like resin. The sheets are cut into smaller pieces and then layered on top of each other. Depending on the performance the manufacturer wants in the stick, materials are layered in different combinations. In some layers, the direction of the threads might go straight up-and-down. In others layers, they're angled. Each stick model has its own formula, and more than 20 layers may be used.

#3
Once the layering is done, the sheets are trimmed and wrapped around a rod, called a "mandrel," to form the shaft. A mold is clamped around the wrapped mandrel, and the composite materials are pressed at a high temperature to form the shaft. Once "cooked," the shaft is removed from the mandrel, smoothed out and placed aside.

#4

Stick blades also are formed from composite lay-ups. Blades usually aren't completely hollow, however. Depending on the stick model, the blades may contain internal reinforcements called "bridges," as well as foams to soften the puck feel.

#5

The blades are placed in molds that heat and press them into final shape. Before the blade is molded, the bottom end of the shaft, called the "hosel," is inserted into the blade. When the blade is molded, it's pressed and heated together with the shaft to form the entire stick.

#6

Once the stick has been formed, excess resin and small imperfections are smoothed out by hand and using tools. Companies will sometimes splash on color to create a specific look. All add lettering and a logo.

#7

A clear protective coating is sprayed on the stick. The coating might be smooth or have a "grip" texture that helps the player hold the stick on the ice.

#8

Before they're shipped, sticks are inspected and undergo tough testing.

HOW ARE GOALIE MASKS MADE?

FIND OUT HOW THE MASKED MARAUDERS IN NET KEEP THEIR MUGS PROTECTED

BY MATT CARLSON

Goaltenders didn't even wear masks until Hall-of-Famer Jacques Plante famously bucked tradition in 1959. Before long, nearly all goalies wore masks made from fiberglass, a hard material made using poisonous chemicals. The workers who made them had to wear masks themselves to avoid breathing dangerous fumes! "That's how masks were made for a long time," said Mark Gignac, senior category manager – goalie at Bauer Hockey.

Nowadays, making goalie masks is a lot less messy, and masks are getting lighter and protect goalies better because they're made from composites – the same tough stuff used to make sticks that help players shoot harder.

Goalie masks have three main parts: the outside shell, the wire cage and an inside lining system. Here's how they're made:

THE SHELL

#1
Different types of composite materials are pressed into large sheets, like huge pieces of plastic wrapping paper only much stronger.
The sheets are layered by hand on top of each other in a specific pattern, almost like following cooking recipe.

#2
The layers of sheets are sliced into flat, cookie-cutter forms of the shell, called the "kit."
A glue is combined with the kit, which is then placed into a mold. There it gets cooked under pressure at temperatures up to 400 degrees Fahrenheit to create the hard mask shell.

#3
The shell is sanded and a computerized tool trims it precisely to size. After that, the shell is painted in a plain color or a paint schemes.

THE CAGE

#4
The mask's wire cage is made at a special factory where metal is treated, cut, bent and welded together. The wire cage may be polished, painted or even sandblasted.

#5
The wire cage is then tested at the factory so it meets safety standards.

GOALTENDERS DIDN'T EVEN WEAR MASKS UNTIL HALL-OF-FAMER JACQUES PLANTE FAMOUSLY BUCKED TRADITION IN 1959

THE LINER

#6

Inside the mask's shell are foams, straps and other pieces that add protection and provide a comfortable fit to the goalie's head. The foams are precisely cut to fit into spaces in a carefully designed lining system. Every piece of foam is in the right place for a reason – to protect the goalie.

#7

In some masks, the liner actually floats a tiny distance from the shell for even more protection.

#8

Once the shell, cage and liner are ready, workers on an assembly line put all the components together following exact instructions.

ASSEMBLY & TESTING

#9

An inspector at the end of the line makes sure everything was put together correctly. Some masks in every batch are tested to Canadian and U.S. standards, and to equipment makers' own standards.

#10

The masks then are shipped to hockey stores, goalies themselves or to an artist who can paint a goaltender's personal design on the mask. A finished pro-quality mask weights just under 2.5 pounds.

MADE TO ORDER? Goalies can pay more to customize parts of their mask. Measurements can be taken of the goalie's face and head, and the lining system can be made to fit him or her perfectly. Sometimes goalies will request a special wire pattern for the mask to give them the exact view they want.

HOW ARE GOALIE MASKS DESIGNED?

MEET THE MAN BEHIND THE COOLEST LOOKING LIDS IN THE LEAGUE
BY MATT CARLSON

Y ou can't see much of a goaltender's face through his mask, but his expression is on display.

Masks just don't just protect goaltenders. The elaborate paint schemes on the outer shells are works of art that reveal netminders' personalities and tell stories.

David Gunnarsson, a self-described "old-school artist" and "sports nerd," works in the small town of Savsjo, Sweden, and paints masks for the world's top goalies. He's the go-to guy for premier puckstoppers like Henrik Lundqvist and Carey Price, and many who hope to become that good. "Goalies are very special people, as you know, and that fits me like a glove," said Gunnarsson, whose studio is partly in a barn where his grandfather once kept cows. "Last year, I painted more than 200 masks and every single mask is totally unique."

Look closely at one of Gunnarsson's masks, even on TV, and you'll see his designs include all sorts of beautiful details. These might be patterns based on team logos and include landmarks and other things associated with a team and its city. Some goalies blend in artistic elements from their nicknames, hometowns and personal interests. Here's how he makes his art come to life for his customers.

#1 Gunnarsson and each goalie talk in person, on the phone and video chats, or via emails. Although he visits North America several times a year, Gunnarsson never has enough time to meet with each goalie personally. He gets a good idea of the theme and style a goalie wants. "It might be scary, funny or very classic," he said.

#2 He then creates mask designs on paper using colored pencils.

#3 Once he finishes his sketches, he emails them to the goalies then makes revisions until everything is just the way the goalie wants it. Once the team also approves the design, it's time to start painting.

#4 Gunnarsson keeps blank, white goalie mask shells from several manufacturers in stock at his studio. The blank shells are first lightly sanded by hand so paint and other elements stick better.

#5 Gunnarsson uses different techniques to paint his designs, but he does most of his work with an airbrush, a tool that sprays paint very precisely. He also uses tiny paintbrushes and sketch pens to create fine detail and texture. He uses water-based paint, not harsh solvent paint, and said his studio "doesn't smell bad."

#6

He usually starts by painting the most intricate elements and then the background. The paint dries quickly at room temperature.

#7

Once a mask dries, Gunnarsson takes photos and makes a video and then sends them to the goalie and team for a final review.

#8

Once everyone is happy, he sprays the mask with several layers of a clear protective coating. This stuff is solvent-based and has a strong odor but is needed to keep the mask from being damaged or chipped by pucks and other impacts on the ice.

#9

Once the coating has dried and any excess is smoothed out, the cage over the goalies' eyes is re-attached.

#10

The masks – just the shell and cage – are then shipped express to the manufacturer in North America. The manufacturer inserts the interior lining, padding and strap systems that allow the mask to fit to the goalie's face and provide critical added protection.

HOW SHOULD KIDS PRACTISE ON THE ICE?

WANT TO LEARN SKILLS LIKE THE PROS? FIRST, HAVE FUN AND PLAY LIKE A KID, THEN WORK YOUR WAY UP TO THE HARD STUFF
BY JARED CLINTON

There's no tried-and-true development method to becoming an NHL star, but every player's journey starts with the first steps on ice. And though it may seem too simple for what is a difficult process to go from a first-year player to a professional hopeful, the future of most standouts can sometimes boil down to the attention to turning those steps into a near perfect stride. Ask Jules Jardine, who has had a hand in the development of Connor McDavid, John Tavares and P.K. Subban, to name a few.

STAGE 1

Jardine, president and chief instructor at World Class Hockey Development, said that an emphasis on skating in the first few years of a young player's development **ages 4 to 8,** can set the base for a successful career to be built upon. "It's funny that in most sports – tennis, golf, those individual sports — there's so much focus on technical correctness," Jardine explained. "When you get into hockey, you see there are not many people doing that. It's very important to build a proper, correct, technical stride at a young age, and that will stay with you forever."

STAGE 2

It's not until the skating stride is down that development in the second stage, **ages 9 to 11,** can really begin. At those ages, development needs to continue to focus on skating, but Jardine said individual basics and technical skills – puck control, passing, receiving, shooting – can be worked in. The greatest separator at this age, according to Corey McNabb, director of Hockey Canada's development programs, is being able to move freely about the ice. "It's still a lot of skating, more trying to develop quickness, speed and power, but really working on acceleration, change of direction and agility," McNabb said. "That's really the focus at that level."

STAGE 3

As young players reach the third stage of their development, ages **12 to 15,** the broader individual skills can be addressed. Players should be focusing on understanding proper positioning, coverages and how to transition from offense to defense, while developing the ability to protect the puck and read the ice. "That's going to come more in the third age group, where someone's going to come and get you and you have the vision to put it on someone's tape," Jardine said. "You know where everyone is on the ice, like a Gretzky-type thing."

HAVE FUN! No matter what stage of development, though, Jardine said there has to be close attention paid to the game's mental aspects. The game should be fun, and coaches and parents alike should make it clear mistakes are going to made at every level. "That mental part is very, very important," Jardine said, "because if you take it away, kids are just going to hate the game."

STAGE 4

The development of the puck handling ability that separates superstars from utility players can come in once a player reaches **16 years old or more.** Those in their late-teens should be refining their puck skills through repetition, McNabb said, and learning to shoot, receive and complete passes and stick handle without loss of speed. But Jardine acknowledged that players should also be honest and recognize their specialties. "You can play at a very high level doing a few things very well," Jardine added. "So you can try to figure out what kind of player you are. Focus on that, do it the best and you can go very far in hockey."

SKILL DRILLS

AGES 4-8
DRILL: Cross-Ice Hockey

Split the rink into three sections and play wall-to-wall hockey with nets. "Kids see hockey on TV and they see a game, and they want to play some version of that," McNabb said. "The rink is down to their size, there are more kids involved, they're changing direction more often, they're handling the puck, they're getting more shots on net."

AGES 9-11
DRILL: 4 Pylon Agility

"Go as fast as you can in any direction, but you have to go around all four pylons," McNabb said. "You want to start to see some randomness, some change in direction, maybe fake to one and go to another. You start to encourage their creativity." **FIGURE 1**

AGES 12-15
DRILL: Quick Feet – Pass Off The Wall

"The forward has to work on picking the puck up, quick feet, acceleration and crossovers," McNabb said. "A defenseman has to mirror. It's control skating, pivoting, backward crossovers, stick position. It's a really good drill." **FIGURE 2**

AGES 16 AND OVER
DRILL: Stride Jumps, Squats

"Stride jump side to side with weight as far as you can go," Jardine said. "Squats you're obviously going to get into the weight as well. I always tell my kids, look at any NHL hockey player – they have a big base and big legs."

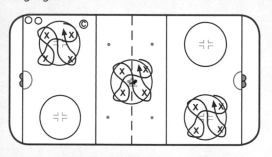

FIGURE 1

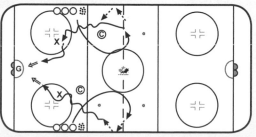

FIGURE 2

HOW SHOULD KIDS TRAIN OFF THE ICE?

FOR YOUNGSTERS WANTING TO WORK OUT LIKE THE PROS, THE KEYS ARE FORM, FLEXIBILITY AND PLAYING MORE THAN JUST HOCKEY

BY RONNIE SHUKER

At Ben Prentiss' gym in Darien, Conn., the list of guys working out reads like an All-Star Game lineup: Max Pacioretty, Matt Moulson, James van Riemsdyk, Kevin Shattenkirk and Jonathan Quick. But there are others, not as pumped, nor as chiselled, but just as driven and motivated, even though they're less than half the age of some of the NHL stars they're training to become. "We have kids come in at 12," Prentiss said. "Some are so focused and intense, it's scary."

Contrary to what most people think, it's safe and even beneficial for kids to train – and train hard – as long as their bodies are ready for the workouts. Though there's no hard-and-fast rule as to which age they can get the green light to begin, Prentiss recommends waiting until after kids hit puberty. Once their bodies have matured to that point, they're free to start training without worrying about hurting the prime growth period in their teenaged years. "Research has shown that it actually strengthens their bones and helps them grow," said Prentiss, head trainer and owner of Prentiss Hockey Performance. "Not in terms of height, but in terms of a healthy body."

Prentiss said it's a myth that kids can stunt their growth by training too "early," but he does point out several key differences youngsters must keep in mind when working out. They should avoid heavy-load exercises like squats and bench or shoulder press. Bodyweight training and using medicine balls and five-pound empty barbells are better, because there's no risk of putting too much weight on the spine. The focus should be on form, flexibility and especially variety, doing eight to 12 repetitions (15 maximum) and just two sets per exercise.

For a sport that Wayne Gretzky famously claimed is 90 percent mental, kids who want to work out like the stars must understand training isn't all about the body. It's easy to get caught up in the physical side, but Prentiss emphasizes the importance of preparing the brain for the body's hard work ahead. "Some kids can handle the demands of working out, lifting weights, handling instructions, the seriousness of it," he said. "And then some kids come in and think it's Romper Room or babysitting."

Finally, and this may shock many parents, kids shouldn't focus only on hockey. By playing too much at such a young age, they can get injuries that NHL players get like hernias and torn labrums – injuries that happen because they repeat the same motion, like skating, too much. Playing other sports will exercise and develop other muscles. "When I tell parents, 'Hey, little Johnny should be playing sports other than hockey,' they look at me like I have five heads," Prentiss said. "Kids need to develop a base of athleticism and a change in the muscle patterns. Let them be athletic, let them use muscles in different ways other than skating. That, in turn, is going to help their longevity in terms of playing hockey."

"RESEARCH HAS SHOWN THAT TRAINING ACTUALLY STRENGTHENS KIDS' BONES AND HELPS THEM GROW."

BEN PRENTISS, STRENGTH AND CONDITIONING COACH

HOW MUCH HOCKEY SHOULD KIDS PLAY?

PARENTS: WANT YOUR KIDS TO GET BETTER AT THE GAME? HAVE THEM PLAY LESS HOCKEY – AND MORE SPORTS INSTEAD

BY RONNIE SHUKER

Ben Prentiss sees it all the time. Parents come in to his Connecticut gym and expect him to put their child on a path to becoming one of the many NHL stars he trains during the off-season. What they don't know is that a lot of the training for his NHL clients doesn't involve hockey. In the summer, his guys don't even hit the ice until late July or early August.

Hockey may be a year-round job for NHL players, but it shouldn't be for kids. It actually hurts their development in two ways: it decreases their overall athleticism, and it increases the likelihood of typical hockey injuries like hip and groin problems. "That's a big, big, big problem now," Prentiss said. "These kids, who are 12 to 15, they're playing 70 games a year…All they do is play hockey. They don't get their feet out of skates, they play too many games and they develop an overuse injury."

To prevent this, Prentiss gets his pre-teen and early teen clients to play other sports. The best ones require different muscles while increasing mobility and flexibility. He even has his NHL clients do non-hockey workouts. At the beginning of their off-season, he has them do gymnastics-type exercises to work muscles they don't usually use.

Daniel Noble sees the all-hockey all-the-time parental philosophy far too often as well. And like Prentiss, he adds other sports into training. He had Maple Leafs first-rounder Mitch Marner playing handball and badminton, and both of the Ritchie brothers (Brett and Nick) were dedicated tennis players. "Overspecialization is a big problem in hockey," said Noble, director of athlete performance at the Hill Academy in Toronto. "We have kids as young as seven, eight years old and they can't even throw a baseball."

It sounds strange, but having kids play more sports will actually help them specialize in hockey down the road. Tyler Goodale, for one, has seen the benefits of being a multi-sport athlete firsthand. In the off-season, he trains Jamie Benn, who played high-level baseball throughout his teens until hockey eventually took over. "Playing baseball was huge for him," said Goodale, strength and conditioning coach at the Canadian Sports Institute. "He improved his hand-eye coordination, his strength from swinging the bat and throwing the ball. He was also running, and running speed correlates really strongly with skating speed."

Goodale suggests a different number of sports depending on age: one or two sports for 17- to 19-year-olds, three sports for 13- to 16-year-olds, four for nine- to 12-year-olds and as many as six for three- to nine-year-olds.

VARIETY IS THE SPICE OF LIFE,
SAY TOP TRAINERS. THESE ARE FOUR SPORTS KIDS SHOULD BE PLAYING IN THE SUMMER

LACROSSE

"It's hand-eye coordination, it's a different movement and its playable surface is big," Noble said. "The problem with hockey is you're always on the ice, so it really affects the ankles, because the foot's always locked in a skate. It's important to get out of the skate to let the ankle work and do what it's supposed to."

SWIMMING

"Swimming is probably the best because of the aerobic capacity of it," Prentiss said. "There's no stress on the joints, and you're doing something completely different."

SOCCER

"Soccer's the only one where you have to develop that foot-eye coordination," Goodale said. "It's non-contact, and it's a good way to just develop a lot of different skill sets."

GYMNASTICS

"Things like monkey bars and rope climbing are very prehistoric in nature," Prentiss said. "But that's what our genetic makeup is made for – climbing, pulling, rowing, tumbling. It's about primal movement patterns, not letting kids use machines and locking their body in and more letting them move: throw medicine balls, pull ropes, those kinds of things."

SOLUTIONS

ANAHEIM DUCKS

```
P A N I K N N O S B I G N
C A M F O W L E R R R M R I
Q R G R E L S E K D S E J
F C K G S L L A O S R B K
L C O R E Y P E R R Y R G
Z L O G L T D H N H A E O
K N R R L E Z O H V R V X
E R A K T I S L L A R F A
G C A O T N A L A B U L T
Y V A T A N E N E F M I A
B W S M K K F F O Y N S R
H O N D A C E N T E R T C
C U J R L I N D H O L M E
```

QUIZ
1 The Mighty Ducks of Anaheim; 2 The Walt Disney Company; 3 The Norris Trophy; 4 Football; 5 Teemu Selanne; 6 Ottawa; 7 Andrew Cogliano; 8 William Jennings Trophy; 9 Chicago.

BY THE NUMBERS
22

FILL IN THE BLANKS
TAMPA BAY, VANCOUVER, ARIZONA, CAROLINA and CALGARY. **Player = PERRY**

ARIZONA COYOTES

```
S D O M I N G U E R T O R
N E N N E H C S K K M E E
N I R I E D E R A C S N I
U P K L R E A X N Y E E R
R P F S L Y D T L W K K A
H E Y O O O L A A M R A L
C T E M M G E E R B O R I
Y T N I B I I R S S R O G
H A T N O I G L S S L V N
C N S H A N E D O A N D R
R E C D M O D N N G O E B
L W I E H T I M S E K I M
```

QUIZ
1 True; 2 2003; 3 Wayne Gretzky; 4 Dallas; 5 Three; 6 Brayden; 7 Score a goal; 8 Oliver Ekman-Larsson; 9 Tie Domi.

BY THE NUMBERS
97

FILL IN THE BLANKS
RED WINGS, DEVILS, SENATORS, SABRES, FLAMES and DUCKS. **Player = DVORAK**

BOSTON BRUINS

```
S T K N E D R A G D T S Z
W N E S H R A K A T U J A
E K E F A M A D V I U X R
E N R L L N O N A N K E A
N C L E R T E A T U K K S
E A S T J W G H R K A E C
Y Y S Y D C R C A S R K S
N A P K D D I R N O A U S
P I O L B I A A O S S E G
E U O C I A S M R T K P W
L B N A H M K S H C I E U
G I E E K U B O A E H U J
N O R E G R E B D C D L N
```

QUIZ
1 6-foot-9; 2 New York Islanders and Ottawa Senators; 3 Brad Marchand; 4 66; 5 Don Cherry; 6 TD Garden; 7 Nine; 8 Malcolm; 9 Prince Edward Island.

BY THE NUMBERS
60 percent

FILL IN THE BLANKS
CHICAGO, WASHINGTON, DALLAS, MONTREAL and NASHVILLE. **Player = CHARA**

BUFFALO SABRES

```
S D T R A H N I E R T R E
N E L N T I L D E K M E B
E V E O A V I N L U I T A
N A Y S S D H J O C S N C
I N R L R E K B H J E E C
A D F U L Y C E N W G C M
L E Y O N I L A A M R K I
O R E M L N E E M H O N V
T K N T B I O R S S G A Q
S A T N O I G H O S L B N
I N O G I L B N I A E Y R
R E C D M U D N O M O E B
S T H E D O K P O S O K H
```

QUIZ
1 Pittsburgh; 2 Los Angeles and Anaheim; 3 Brian Gionta; 4 Ryan and Cal; 5 Robin Lehner; 6 KeyBank Center; 7 Zemgus Girgensons; 8 Atlanta Thrashers; 9 Jake McCabe.

BY THE NUMBERS
1,757

FILL IN THE BLANKS
CHICAGO, WINNIPEG, BOSTON, TORONTO, OTTAWA and LAS VEGAS. **Player = GIONTA**

CALGARY FLAMES

```
E E G A U D R E A U T A Z
L M N A J A T S R D R J E
L O G N A R C E N A K X T
I D A L L O W A O I P T Z
O E E M R U L A L Y K R O
T L A A O R M O N A H A N
T D H R E A R H C U A K A
A D B F O F A H H I M R D
N A Z T U L U G C S I L R
E S B A C K L U N D L P O
F B O A J L K E A A T C I
Y E K C O H Y N N H O J G
C K U A N I F E D O N L R
```

QUIZ
1 Las Vegas; 2 Dynamo; 3 Scotiabank; 4 Two of Ottawa, Colorado and St. Louis; 5 Keith Tkachuk; 6 'Johnny Hockey'; 7 Lacrosse; 8 Chicago; 9 Special Olympics.

BY THE NUMBERS
11.67

FILL IN THE BLANKS
GOLDEN KNIGHTS, CANUCKS, BLUES, ISLANDERS, OILERS, SABRES, PANTHERS and DUCKS. **Player = GAUDREAU**

CAROLINA HURRICANES

```
E S C W B B F L E M A S U
S I A N E R A C N P T R I
J C M S E E T R Y A E E V
K N W T L T K X A H N T R
R A A E E T I L H S R E T
T R R M S P D B U A K P Y
I F D P U E E N C A C L N
O N U N I S N E H E F L O
S O R I L C K O S P U I S
A R I A R E N N I K S B C
M P V K U L I N D H O L M
C I R M S X A E R I N S I
N E N E N I A V A R E T E
```

QUIZ
1 Detroit; 2 First; 3 Jeff Skinner; 4 Calder Trophy; 5 Sebastian Aho; 6 Pittsburgh; 7 Jim Rutherford; 8 He's a dentist; 9 Whalers.

BY THE NUMBERS
13.67

FILL IN THE BLANKS
BOSTON, OTTAWA, NASHVILLE, CHICAGO and CALGARY. **Player = STAAL**

CHICAGO BLACKHAWKS

```
P A N I K N I R A N A P N
L C E O L E J A S R M A I
J R G N I L R A D D S T B
F A K C S L G A O S R R K
L W O R K I I A O C V I U
O F O A O V D H N H O C H
S O R D P E O H H M M K E
A R B K T N N T I A I K R
Z R E T N E C D E T I N U
E W S D K U F F I Z N E R
S E T N E Q S E L P A T S
C H J A L M A R S S O N E
```

QUIZ
1 Denis Savard; 2 One; 3 Patrick Kane; 4 Jonathan Toews;
5 Duncan Keith; 6 Corey Crawford; 7 Pittsburgh and
Detroit; 8 Nick Schmaltz; 9 Chicago.

BY THE NUMBERS
52

FILL IN THE BLANKS
NEW YORK, PHILADELPHIA, PITTSBURGH,
BOSTON and NASHVILLE. **Player = KEITH**

COLORADO AVALANCHE

```
L M N I M E H C U A E B N
L A E O L E N E H C U D I
J Z N T H E C H I N F C C
S Z A D M A C K I N N O N
O I T D E U A A R S W L S
D N N A O S P I C K A R D
E E A D E R K H J A H A O
R S R O I R O O I E U N R
B I J O T S H V G P P D E
E U R E T N E C I S P E P
R B E D S O F F I L C B R
G E B O U R Q U E P A T S
C A N D R I G H E T T O F
```

QUIZ
1 Quebec City; 2 Two; 3 Canada's Sports Hall of Fame;
4 19; 5 Pepsi; 6 Jared Bednar; 7 First; 8 Gold; 9 Malmo.

BY THE NUMBERS
16

FILL IN THE BLANKS
PHILADELPHIA, ANAHEIM, WINNIPEG,
EDMONTON, MONTREAL, LAS VEGAS,
NEW YORK, SAN JOSE and WASHINGTON.
Player = LANDESKOG

COLUMBUS BLUE JACKETS

```
N E G A N I J S A W E N Z
O W E N N B E R G D K J E
S O D N A R N L N U K X T
N D I N O S N I K T A E V
H E W W E R E N S K I H D
O F N N O I R O O A E A U
J T O R T O R E L L A R B
D J I L S F J S T S W T I
O R T O I L E G Y S I N N
K S A A E G T E M D L E S
T B N V H N E R K S L L K
Y E K N A S E O A H C L Y
M U D Y K S V O R B O B E
```

QUIZ
1 A Union soldier during the American Civil War;
2 Tampa Bay; 3 Mike Foligno; 4 Cam Atkinson;
5 Syria; 6 Sergei Bobrovsky; 7 Insurance; 8 Anchorage;
9 Edmonton.

BY THE NUMBERS
2

FILL IN THE BLANKS
BUFFALO, MONTREAL, DALLAS, PITTSBURGH,
CHICAGO, CAROLINA and COLUMBUS.
Player = FOLIGNO

DALLAS STARS

```
H A S I N P N O S B E E N
C A M F G H L S P R M I G
Q H J A M I E B E N N H R
F C I G S N L A Z G R C E
A S O T E D P E Z R U T B
K E D G C Y P R A H S I G
S V R M L H O O H V R R N
A A L K T U C L L E R F I
I E T O S C A O R B U L L
Y M A S A U E O C F M I K
B N E N O T H E L K N S W
H L N I A S I U H M A H S
C U J R N I N Z C A L J E
```

QUIZ
1 Ken Hitchcock; 2 1999; 3 Youth model; 4 Ottawa;
5 Tyler Seguin; 6 Jamie Benn; 7 Patrick Sharp;
8 Kari Lehtonen; 9 Antoine Roussel.

BY THE NUMBERS
583

FILL IN THE BLANKS
SABRES, ISLANDERS, RED WINGS and
GOLDEN KNIGHTS. **Player = BENN**

DETROIT RED WINGS

```
A T H A N A S I O U T A Z
A N E D E K E Y S E R J E
B T G N A R C B L A B X T
D N A L L O H L O N I E Z
E P E M R N K A K Y W R E
L A A A O W M S N Q E A T
K E H D F A R H E U H K T
A E T K S L A I H I U R E
D I N O B L Z L C S A L R
E U A A H Y E L R T K P B
R B M A V L K E A A E C E
K I W D M U H T M M O L R
H T I G N I N E D N E L G
```

QUIZ
1 Detroit's old arena; 2 Little Caesar's Arena; 3 25; 4 12;
5 Denmark; 6 Steve Yzerman; 7 France; 8 Mike Babcock;
9 Gordie Howe, Ted Lindsay and Sid Abel.

BY THE NUMBERS
62

FILL IN THE BLANKS
ARIZONA, WINNIPEG, EDMONTON, MINNESOTA,
LAS VEGAS, DETROIT, COLUMBUS, MONTREAL,
TORONTO and CALGARY. **Player = ZETTERBERG**

EDMONTON OILERS

```
C D E Y S R E U M S T A A
T O B L A T M A C N M R C
I D E N R E I F L I E U K
N A R M O B F E L K C T I
A I E U E G C S N O R E L
L V Y B R A K L N H A R E
L A R S S O N O I T I F R
E D N T P E O Y S N S L A
L C X Z L R U H C E A R I
C M O G A P O O D G I J H
M I C M C U H N L U T L C
U L G R E T Z K Y N L N H
```

QUIZ
1 Toronto; 2 Germany; 3 Art Ross Trophy; 4 Sidney
Crosby; 5 Detroit; 6 True; 7 4; 8 Ryan Nugent-Hopkins;
9 Taylor Hall.

BY THE NUMBERS
30

FILL IN THE BLANKS
TAMPA BAY, VANCOUVER, EDMONTON,
DALLAS, NASHVILLE, ARIZONA and FLORIDA.
Player = MCDAVID

FLORIDA PANTHERS

```
M T K L N E N I K O J R Z
A N R U E R A C A T S E G
S Q E O A M E B L I B T N
E L M N L H O L E N I N O
I C I G C D A L B K E E S
Y A E O O W G S Y Q E C E
M A R C H E S S A U L T H
S T N K O D Y N R I R & T
R I D D B P A O C S E B A
E U N A L E W L R T M B M
M E I Z N E K C A M I E W
E I W E K U B O Z C Y E K
D T R G A J R I M O R A J
```

QUIZ

1 Miami; 2 Tom Rowe; 3 Tampa Bay; 4 Aaron Ekblad;
5 Arizona; 6 Toronto; 7 45; 8 Shootouts; 9 Roberto Luongo.

BY THE NUMBERS

3 times

FILL IN THE BLANKS

DEVILS, CANUCKS, SABRES, ISLANDERS, CAPITALS
and CANADIENS. **Player = EKBALD**

LOS ANGELES KINGS

```
Q M P Y A T R G M Y T A N
L U E O L U J A T R M R I
J Z I T H E C H L N F C C
E Z B C S S G A B O R I K
F I E R K U I A R S W L S
F N V A O Y D B N R E O H
C E I D P W O H A A H F O
A S N K I R N E I E U F R
R I N O T S O R S P P O E
T U V V A Y U H C S K T T
E B E D R O F F I L C S R
R E T N E C S E L P A T S
C T I P A D I M B E N T Q
```

QUIZ

1 Two; 2 Ben Bishop; 3 6-foot-7; 4 Jonathan Quick;
5 Columbus and Philadelphia; 6 Calgary; 7 Yugoslavia;
8 Lakers and Clippers; 9 Salt Lake City.

BY THE NUMBERS

28 minutes

FILL IN THE BLANKS

COLUMBUS, ARIZONA, BOSTON, NEW YORK
and TORONTO. **Player = BROWN**

MINNESOTA WILD

```
R X C E L E N E R G Y G E
E D N T I H C S E K M R L
T T E S A V I H T M I A I
I I R T E D J R U C S N I
E N O E G R U P S Y E L V
R P F W S U D T N W K U N
R E Y A O I A A A M R N I
E T E R M A R E Y B E D M
D D N T L I M A R S K O O
E U T N O I G L P D C V P
I M I K K O K O I V U D R
N B C D V U D Q N G Z O H
L A I E H K Y N B U D I B
```

QUIZ

1 'Gabby'; 2 Finland; 3 Marc, Jordan and Jared; 4 Carolina;
5 Fifth; 6 A silver in 2010; 7 Bill Masterton Trophy;
8 True; 9 Buffalo.

BY THE NUMBERS

plus-90

FILL IN THE BLANKS

ISLANDERS, BRUINS, SABRES, AVALANCHE,
FLYERS and GOLDEN KNIGHTS. **Player = DUBNYK**

MONTREAL CANADIENS

```
S P B Y A T R G M Q T A M
L N E I L U J A E R M R I
A E R T N G C L X E B C T
E A G A R D D L R B I E C
C P E M R Y K A C E W N H
I A V A O S D G N W E A E
R E I R N U K H A A H K L
P S N K L N M E I E U E L
Y I N O B S O R S H P L Q
E U V V H Y U H C S K P T
R B E A U L I E U A E C R
A I W D M U H N L M O L O
C T I P A C I O R E T T Y
```

QUIZ

1 24; 2 Claude Julien; 3 Bill Masterton Trophy;
4 Once (1980); 5 21,000; 6 Maurice; 7 10; 8 P.K. Subban;
9 Baseball.

BY THE NUMBERS

33, Patrick Roy

FILL IN THE BLANKS

PHILADELPHIA, LAS VEGAS, CHICAGO,
WINNIPEG, EDMONTON, DETROIT, MONTREAL,
TORONTO, OTTAWA and NEW YORK.
Player = PACIORETTY

NASHVILLE PREDATORS

```
B T J L N K E E W O S R N
A L R A E P N M L O H K E
Z A E O M N O B L I R T S
E V M N I E T I E N Y N N
N I I R K D S L L K A E A
O O E O E G E N Y E N C H
S L R C F R G S E U E N O
S E N K I E D N R A L A J
D T O D S B I O C S L B A
I T N A H S R S R T I B M
V E I Z E R B T A M S U W
R I W E R O M A N J O S I
A T R G A F R W M E G A J
```

QUIZ

1 Music City; 2 Washington; 3 Carolina; 4 Philadelphia;
5 Shea Weber; 6 Carrie Underwood; 7 Bern; 8 Power play
goals; 9 He was named MVP.

BY THE NUMBERS

75 percent

FILL IN THE BLANKS

FLYERS, RED WINGS, ISLANDERS, BLACKHAWKS,
RANGERS and STARS. **Player = FISHER**

NEW JERSEY DEVILS

```
S Z P Y W T N G R Y G A N
L L A H R O L Y A T R R I
J A I C E E O H Y N E S R
E I B S H S G D S O E I E
R T E R E A I A H S N L D
W N V A O V D B E R E O I
C E I G P H E N R I Q U E
O D N K I R N R O E U F N
R U N O T S O C S P P O H
I R E I M L A P C O K T C
E P E D R J F D I L N S S
C A M M A L L E R I A T S
A T I Z O D I R B U N O Y
```

QUIZ

1 Fred Shero; 2 Lou Lamoriello; 3 Michigan State; 4 First;
5 Martin Brodeur; 6 Lance Armstrong; 7 Reverend Tim
Lovejoy; 8 Kyle Palmieri; 9 Bryce Salvador.

BY THE NUMBERS 53 points

FILL IN THE BLANKS

CALGARY, NEW YORK, DETROIT, WINNIPEG,
TORONTO and NASHVILLE. **Player = GREENE**

NEW YORK ISLANDERS

```
Z T K A U B N E P U T S Z
A N E S E R A V A T S J G
S T E N A M C B L I B X A
E N E L L O O L E N I E R
I C L U T T E R B U C K T
D A S A O W G S T Q E A H
E Y R D D A R H E S A K S
N E E K O D A N H I R R N
B I D L B L A A C S E L O
E U N A I A L L R T M P W
R B A A H A K T H G I E W
G I W E K U B O Y C H U K
H T D R E I W E D N C L P
```

QUIZ

1 Nassau Coliseum; **2** Four; **3** Doug Weight; **4** Goalie; **5** Thomas Greiss; **6** First overall; **7** 14; **8** Dennis Seidenberg; **9** Cal Clutterbuck.

BY THE NUMBERS

1,111

FILL IN THE BLANKS

MONTREAL, BUFFALO, NASHVILLE, OTTAWA, ARIZONA, MINNESOTA and BOSTON.
Player = TAVARES

NEW YORK RANGERS

```
N H G A N O D C M N S N Z
R W L U N D Q V I S T J E
S I F R O R C G N U E J S
T E T K S N E N S K A M R
H F L X N B R W O A N I E
E Z U C C A R E L L O L D
G J A L S R S S T S W L I
A R E Q I G E H Y S I E E
R S N A E Y T E M D J R R
D B G V A H N E R K S L K
E E I H A S E O S H O V Y
N U V D G I R A R D I B M
```

QUIZ

1 Montreal and Vancouver; **2** Oslo; **3** Are; **4** Antti Raanta; **5** Mark Messier; **6** Phil Esposito; **7** Dan Girardi, Rick Nash, Marc Staal and Derek Stepan; **8** Michael Grabner; **9** Jonathan Tanner.

BY THE NUMBERS

21

FILL IN THE BLANKS

RED WINGS, STARS, CAPITALS, SABRES, KINGS, FLYERS and SENATORS. **Player = GRABNER**

OTTAWA SENATORS

```
D N O D N O C K P N A M S
B L I E N S I R H C M T I
O T U R R I S A A D O T B
O X R T H I Q A E C V I U
W F A N C V D H U H O C P
I O S A U N H O F F M A N
E J S I O E N T I A G K R
C D A D B N O S R E D N A
K N R A N E C D A T I N U
I O B N K U F U I Z N E R
G T T A Y P M O T T A T S
C H J C L K A R L S S O N
```

QUIZ

1 Yes (1927); **2** Tampa Bay; **3** Jason Spezza; **4** Norris Trophy; **5** His 1,000th game with Ottawa; **6** Canadian Tire Centre; **7** Lacrosse; **8** Brian Elliott; **9** Cody Ceci.

BY THE NUMBERS

5 (5.2 exactly)

FILL IN THE BLANKS

CANUCKS, PANTHERS, FLYERS, AVALANCHE, ISLANDERS, JETS, COYOTES and BRUINS.
Player = KARLSSON

PHILADELPHIA FLYERS

```
Q Z P W B E L L E M A R E
S C H E N N L Y A T R R I
J L I L E H O H Y N E N V
P F C L L A T X E H N O R
R F O S E K I A H S R S G
U A U F O S D B E A I A L
G R T A P T E N C M C M K
O I U R I O N E M E O E O
R U R G T L K O S P U V H
D R I O U L N P C O S E C
M P E D U D F D I L I T S
C A R M S X A E R I N S I
A E R E H E B S I T S O G
```

QUIZ

1 Wayne Simmonds; **2** The semifinals and final of the men's NCAA hockey championship; **3** Three; **4** Mario Lemieux; **5** Steve Mason; **6** Shayne Gostisbehere; **7** Luke Schenn; **8** Bobby Clarke; **9** Wells Fargo Center.

BY THE NUMBERS

34

FILL IN THE BLANKS

SAN JOSE, CAROLINA, COLUMBUS, MINNESOTA, BOSTON, VANCOUVER, FLORIDA, NEW JERSEY.
Player = SIMMONDS

PITTSBURGH PENGUINS

```
S D F Y A R R U M T T A M
T H L N T O L I E K M R C
A D E N A V I L L U S U K
N L U A S D H J Q A I T Y
L P R K R L K B C J W H T
E A Y U O Y C F N W E E S
Y C Y N N I K L A M H R I
C S E I R N M E I H O F V
U I N T B E O Y S L R O Q
P U X Z T L U H C S K R N
G W O G I L B U I A E D R
H I C D M U H N L M O L O
S L I M R C R O S B Y N H
```

QUIZ

1 Cole Harbour; **2** A clothes dryer; **3** Mario Lemieux; **4** Conn Smythe Trophy; **5** A hockey coach; **6** Amanda Kessel; **7** Anaheim and Atlanta; **8** Marc-Andre Fleury; **9** Patric Hornqvist.

BY THE NUMBERS

22

FILL IN THE BLANKS

COLUMBUS, BUFFALO, DETROIT, MONTREAL, CHICAGO and NEW YORK. **Player = MURRAY**

SAN JOSE SHARKS

```
P O V I Q N B M R N C P N
L D R A W L E O J R I A P
B R E N T B U R N S S B A
P A R B S L R S H S A R V
G W U R O I S A O C L O E
O N T A O E L P U H V C L
M O U E P E R C H N M E S
A S O A Y N N E J A I K K
X S C U N O T N R O H T I
U L E T M A R T I N N N U
E R S O K U F E I Z N E R
S A T U A E L R A M A T S
C K J T L M H R D E O N U
```

QUIZ

1 The Shark Tank; **2** Joe Pavelski; **3** Baseball; **4** Joe Thornton; **5** He played with two different teams that year, beginning the season with Boston; **6** Burns Zoo; **7** Patrick Marleau; **8** 500th; **9** Los Angeles.

BY THE NUMBERS

Nearly 4 (3.9 exactly)

FILL IN THE BLANKS

CAPITALS, AVALANCHE, COYOTES, BRUINS, KINGS, LIGHTNING, GOLDEN KNIGHTS and RANGERS. **Player = THORNTON**

ST. LOUIS BLUES

```
P R E T S E E M W U O B N
L C E O L E J A S R M A I
P E R R O N R U D D S T J
O A O K N E S A R A T R A
K E H R K I Y S O D V I K
Y D O A O N E E N H O L E
A A R D T V O U K M M L A
R R B S A N L T I I A L
A T A E T G I S S L M H L
P T R T R E C D T T I S E
S O L E G N A R T E I P N
S C B N E Q S E L P E U S
C S C H W A R T Z S O N Q
```

QUIZ
1 Brett Hull and Adam Oates; 2 Chicago; 3 Mike Yeo; 4 Three (and one silver); 5 Peter Stastny; 6 Football; 7 He was a long-time linesman; 8 Three (their first three seasons); 9 Third, after Rick Nash and Kari Lehtonen.

BY THE NUMBERS
12

FILL IN THE BLANKS
PHILADELPHIA, WINNIPEG, ANAHEIM, DETROIT, ARIZONA, TAMPA BAY, WASHINGTON, CHICAGO, MONTREAL, CALGARY and MINNESOTA.
Player = PIETRANGELO

TAMPA BAY LIGHTNING

```
N A K U C H E R O V S B N
A D N F O T L E R R O H I
M R A R A R T S U S K E J
E O H L S L L A O S M D N
S T P L G L T D T N H T A M
N N L R N D N O H V S N R
I R A K R I R L L A R F E
K C C J O N C O O P E R Z
O V A P L N E N U F M I Y
V W S M L K F F O I N S R
H L N D I C Q N B E N T S
C U Y I K S V E L I S A V
```

QUIZ
1 Steve Yzerman; 2 First (Steve Stamkos); 3 Amalie Arena; 4 New York Rangers; 5 Second; 6 True; 7 A sports agent; 8 The Tonight Show; 9 The city is the continent's lightning capital.

BY THE NUMBERS
77 percent

FILL IN THE BLANKS
PANTHERS, CAPITALS, CANADIENS, FLAMES, BLUE JACKETS, GOLDEN KNIGHTS and BLUES.
Player = STAMKOS

TORONTO MAPLE LEAFS

```
P B K A D R I M C L G A B
N A E N T I L I H K M O C
E D I D Y E P C G T Z A K
F A D E S L H J K A I I Y
L N T R B L K B K S W M D
Z A W S O Y C F Y W E J S
V C Y E P O B U E E H P M
O R E N R A M J L H O A E
R I V X B X L Y M T R Y I
A A X C A M O T E T K Q R
M W O G I B S U I A D E N
O C C D Y M H N L M O G A
K T I P R E D N A L Y N V
```

QUIZ
1 Anaheim; 2 True; 3 New Jersey; 4 Detroit; 5 Alternate captains; 6 Tyler Bozak, Matt Hunwick, Leo Komarov and Morgan Rielly; 7 Wendel Clark; 8 Two; 9 Carolina.

BY THE NUMBERS
67

FILL IN THE BLANKS
EDMONTON, DALLAS, ARIZONA, VANCOUVER, ANAHEIM and TORONTO. **Player = MARNER**

VANCOVUER CANUCKS

```
T E G A R E T T U S E N Z
E S N A J R A N R N K J G
L W O N A I I L N I U L R
M O R T S K R A M W R U A
B R T M H S L N T T K C N
E R A C O S E O O N E A L
N U V R E O E H R I A S U
N B R F S N A E V D W B N
I I O M I L L E R E S I D
N S H A E D M K O S N S A
G R O G E R S A R E N A M
Y E B A E R T S C H I J T
N O P T S Q C E B O M K G
```

QUIZ
1 Willie Desjardins; 2 Henrik; 3 Art Ross Trophy; 4 Brent; 5 Alexandre Burrows; 6 Switzerland; 7 Mikael; 8 Pavel Bure; 9 Mumps.

BY THE NUMBERS
35

FILL IN THE BLANKS
FLORIDA. PITTSBURGH, MONTREAL, EDMONTON, ARIZONA and CAROLINA. **Player = D. SEDIN**

WASHINGTON CAPITALS

```
T E G A N I S K A N E N Z
E J N A J A A N R D K J E
L O O N A R I L N U K X T
G D A S L K N O Z I R E V
A E E M H U L N T N K R W
E L A C O I E O O A E A I
B D E R E T E H R U A R L
A V P F S F A S T I W R L
O I Z O U L P G Y S I L I
K S V A E L L E R D L P A
R Q M A V H K E R A S E M
Y E P N O S S N A H O J S
M O R T S K C A B O N L G
```

QUIZ
1 President's Trophy; 2 15 years; 3 2008; 4 Herb Brooks; 5 T.J. Oshie; 6 False; 7 Marcus Johansson; 8 Conn Smythe Trophy; 9 Jay Beagle.

BY THE NUMBERS
7

FILL IN THE BLANKS
PREDATORS, PANTHERS, CAPITALS, DEVILS and BLACKHAWKS. **Player = ORPIK**

WINNIPEG JETS

```
T E Y E S S I R R O M N Z
R S N A J V A N S N K J Y
B S C H E I F E L E K L R
O O R T S K H A M W C U W
B Y F U G L I E N T Y C O
W R A C E S C O Q A U A L
H U V R E I A O B L D E M
E B S F R M A U P D E B A
E I O U T L O E R P L U D
L S A S E R M K O A L S A
E M O R T S N E I E E A M
R P B A E R T N C H H J T
N O M T S C E N T R E K G
```

QUIZ
1 Atlanta; 2 Andrew Ladd; 3 Carolina; 4 Manitoba Moose; 5 Auston Matthews; 6 Mark Scheifele; 7 Blues; 8 Connor Hellebuyck (CH) 9 Four.

BY THE NUMBERS
5

FILL IN THE BLANKS
FLYERS, AVALANCHE, OILERS, BRUINS and DEVILS. **Player = LAINE**

VEGAS GOLDEN KNIGHTS

```
N H G A N O D C G N S N Z
R W S A G E V S A L T N E
S I F R O R C K L U H J S
N D C I D E N R L L Y T V
T T M O B I L E A R E N A
H F L X G B R W N A L I C
E Z U H C A A E T L O I D
G J T L D R S S T E F L I
A S E A D G E H E I L E E
R S V S E Y T H C D L R R
D E G V E X P A N S I O N
N E I H A C P O S H B V Y
N U V D M I R A R D I B M
```

QUIZ

1 31; **2** Quebec City; **3** Caesars Palace; **4** Nick and Marcus; **5** T-Mobile Arena; **6** Alex Ovechkin; **7** True (Las Vegas Posse); **8** NHL Awards; **9** Black.

BY THE NUMBERS

7¾ times larger

MATCHUP

Calvin Pickard = Colorado
Cody Eakin = Dallas
Tomas Nosek = Detroit
Luca Sbisa = Vancouver
James Neal = Nashville
Brayden McNabb = Los Angeles
William Carrier = Buffalo
Clayton Stoner = Anaheim
Marc-Andre Fleury = Pittsburgh
Nate Schmidt = Washington
Griffin Reinhart = Edmonton
Oscar Lindberg = New York Rangers

PHOTO CREDITS

THANK YOU

Many thanks are due for what
was truly a team effort:

ISABEL TARDIF, for overseeing the entire book.

JASON KAY and **EDWARD FRASER**, for their work behind the scenes.

JESSICA ROSS, for her steady hand throughout the process.

LEANNE GILBERT, for her vision and design.

COLIN ELLIOTT, for meticulously piecing it all together.

Writers **KEN CAMPBELL**, **JARED CLINTON**, **LUKE DECOCK**, **BOB DUFF**,
WAYNE FISH, **RYAN KENNEDY**, **SARAH MCLELLAN**, **AARON PORTZLINE**
and **RANDY SPORTAK**, for their expertise and coverage.

LARRY HUMBER, puzzlemaker extraordinaire,
for bringing the fun in the title.

And, of course, THN's cadre of intrepid interns:
ALEX DEBETS, **CHRIS JONES**,
ISABELLA KRZYKALA and **TAYLOR RETTER**,
for all of their hard work from beginning to end.